Leadership by Engagement has helped me better understand why certain actions or habits of mine have worked or not worked. This book is an easy read with valuable insights and will continue to be a significant reference book in our professional development library. The list of Leadership Engagement Behaviors is in my top desk drawer to keep me on track with my team.

~Maureen Burleson
President -The Montana Group

Leadership by Engagement is the "easy read" which you promised and is full of valuable insights. After my almost 30 years of general management experience, and specific management education, I can say without a doubt there have been times when some of these insights would have smoothed my path if I had been introduced to them in advance rather than learning them through experience. I found chapter six on Harnessing Conflict, and in particular the section on workplace bullying, to be very enlightening.

All in all, there is much in here for any manager to think about and act on, and I plan to re-read it and attempt to put to real use some of the tools, particularly SNIP.

~Peter Budreo
General Manager South Lake CFDC

I love that you start with knowing yourself as the first part of leadership and engagement. So many models and books I've read are about the things to do to become a leader, but your book emphasizes starting with yourself first and starting from the inside. I feel like I can be a better leader after reading this book: by focusing on my intentions and managing "me" more effectively

The data was excellent: I think this information will help leaders influence their leaders that companies need to change the way we lead and manage. Our labour market is changing fast and with the change I think the need for engagement is critical. It's so clear to me that all employees, especially the new Gen Y'ers, need to feel engaged in order to help companies succeed; and that the "old" way of managing is fast becoming detrimental to attraction, retention, engagement and ultimately productivity in the workforce.

~Laura Falby
Director, People Development
Second Cup

The book will be an excellent tool for any new leader to understand the role that they play in creating a healthy and engaged workplace. The research is excellent and hits home the key message that the leader has significant ownership in the engagement process. The book was very easy to read and follow.

~Patrick McCann
Training Director
Wendy's Restaurants of Canada

Every new leader should spend some time with Kathleen's book. Learning to embrace and grow your own character, and then that of your team, is a foundational piece of sound leadership.

~**Peggy Grall**
Canada's Change Coach

This book is written in a manner that compels me to frequently evaluate and compare my own management style and activity to one of ensuring positive engagement with my staff. I am also gratified to discover that it is by accident, and not any special planning, that I happen to apply many of your engagement principles in my day-to-day management of my staff and business. I find it to be one of the most readable management related books I have encountered. Your process of introducing the theory of a principle and then distilling it down to a very practical application makes for very understandable and easy reading. Not dry and tedious at all.

~**Murray A. Child, CFP, R.F.P.**
President
MDK/Child Financial Advisors

Engagement is what companies strive for. The character model in this book provides a roadmap on how to fill the gap between a survey results to achieving an engaged workplace.

~**Bob Bowman**
Plant Manager, Labatt Brewery, Halifax

Some very powerful insights into engagement, trust and the impact of our behaviors. With the willingness to change, some hard work, a little patience and truly listening to others we can transform ourselves not only into better leaders but better individuals as well.

~**Dan Whitley**
Manager
Siemens Canada Limited

True leaders are active. They take hold of what needs to be done and influence the outcome: by clarifying to their people what is expected of them, by having the courage to deliver positive and constructive feedback, and by modeling best practices to cultivate the mutual trust necessary for lasting success. Leaders know they must continually improve to achieve success. First step should be reading *Leadership by Engagement* and then putting into practice the ideas and models it so effectively and engagingly presents to the busy leader of today's workplace.

~**John Walker**
Dean, Faculty of Hospitality & Tourism
George Brown College
Toronto, Ontario.

Leadership by Engagement

Leading Through Authentic Character to Attract, Retain, and Energize

Kathleen Redmond

Engagement Publishing
2009 Toronto, Canada

Leadership by Engagement ~ Leading Through Authentic Character to
Attract, Retain, and Energize
Copyright ©2009 by Kathleen Redmond

Kathleen Redmond
Centre for Character Leadership
1111 Davis Drive
Unit 1, Suite 174
Newmarket, Ontario L3Y 9E5
kr@centreforcharacterleadership.com www.centreforcharacterleadership.com

Library and Archives Canada Cataloguing in Publication
Redmond, Kathleen, 1952-
Leadership by Engagement : Leading Through Authentic Character
to Attract, Retain, and Energize / Kathleen Redmond. -- 2nd ed.
Includes bibliographical references.
ISBN 978-0-9734038-7-9
1. Leadership. 2. Character. I. Title.
HD57.7.R42 2009   658.4'092   C2009-900414-3

ISBN 978-0-9734038-7-9

Edited by Tom Kernaghan
CommuniCritters Cartoons by Patricia Storms
Cover Photos: iStock Photos
Copyright©2009 Centre for Character Leadership Licensors all rights reserved.

Printed in Canada

Disclaimer: Names have been changed to protect confidentiality.

Dedication

Bernard A. Redmond
(1925–2002)

As a Prince Edward Island farm child, an infantryman at 17 years old in WWII and a HVAC Salesman my father exemplified hard work and commitment. He provided a wonderful example of the power and importance of engagement.

Acknowledgements

Tom Kernaghan	Tom's reputation as a writer is excellent, and he is a person of solid, honorable character. Tom has been more than an editor. He has honed, threaded and smoothed the content, researched when we had a gap, interviewed leaders for Intentional Acts of Character, and kept us going when the going got tough. His humor made the journey more fun. He could not have been more engaged or more dedicated to creating a meaningful book.
Cindy Capobianco	Cindy has been the rock in the eye of the storm. Cindy kept track of the rewrites, versions, and research – completing some of the research herself. Cindy's character emerged strongly when she would say "no, enough is enough" when our continuous revisions made it necessary to rest and laugh at ourselves.
Editing/Graphic team	Thank you to Melissa Augusto for her copy editing and proofreading, Adrienne Kiric for graphics and Patricia Storms for the wonderful critters.
Carina Fiedeldey-Van Dijk, PhD	Kudos to Carina for her insights, content edits, and direction. Carina's education and experience in the Emotional Intelligence realm was critical in developing the Character Model.
Leader Contributors	Many generous colleagues, clients and leader friends contributed their perspective and shared their wisdom: Peggy Grall, Laura Falby, Colin W. Moore, Pat McCann, Rick Dominico, Lucille King, Virginia Hackson, Alison Buchanan, Christine DeHaas, Denise Lam, Marni Blouin, Scott Murray, Trish Hewitt, Dan Whitley, Ghislaine Boulianne, John Ryerson, Janet Vanderklugt, Keith Postill, Randall Craig, Sharon Bar-David, Darlene Klemchuk, Johanna Vandenbogaerde, Marci Segal and Paul Gannage.
Terry Russell	Terry has been his usual patient, encouraging and realistic self in the last two years we have been working on this book. He is a great sounding board as he lives in the leadership world and I wholeheartedly trust his judgment. I am so blessed I married a man of such wonderful character.

Contents

Foreword

I have known Kathleen for over a decade. She has been a client, a volunteer in a previous community where I served as Chief Administrative Officer, a volunteer in the Character Community Movement, a trainer/facilitator with two leadership teams that I was and am proud to lead, and our Executive Coach.

Let me tell you a bit about Kathleen and her work. Her character is one of contribution, collaboration, and integrity. Her intention and focus is to do the right thing.

Kathleen supports leaders in creating a workplace with the maximum opportunity for results.

Together we have worked to improve communication and mutual understanding within two organizations. Our team has attended workshops, participated in facilitated discussions, and experienced one-to-one coaching based on the Leadership by Engagement 360 Degree Assessment. Among the benefits we have experienced is a deeper self-understanding and leadership cohesion.

Our senior leaders are talking more to each other and their staff, listening more profoundly, and crafting creative solutions. We support each other more effectively, have tools to reflect upon and consequently our trust levels have increased.

This new book builds on the first book, *Rules of Engagement for Communicating at Work*, which was a handbook for the workforce. *Leadership by Engagement* is a sound and interesting guideline for leaders who choose to develop a highly functioning, engaged team, as well as enjoyable and productive workplace.

Using the Character Model to cultivate inside-out leadership is in my opinion, the only way to create sustainable and effective engagement in a team. Our leaders are working with the framework and we apply it in our decisions and significant interactions.

I highly recommend the book and the author as part of your leadership resources.

John S. Rogers
Chief Administrative Officer
Town of Aurora

Leadership is a well-researched concept that has received considerable attention since the nineties. In this book, readers are invited to see themselves as true leaders, because in reality leaders can be found at all levels of employment – they don't necessarily have to be managers. Leaders influence and inspire; managers are merely in a superior position in the organization.

However, at the very least, in the workplace all managers are expected to be leaders. Effective managers do demonstrate leadership capabilities. Yet managerial status does not guarantee leadership. Managers tend to control, while leaders have authority earned by their ability to be observant of and sensitive towards such situations, and by creating a constructive atmosphere of mutual confidence and loyalty. For Kathleen Redmond the reason for this difference is that authentic character lies at the heart of leadership, and thereby provides engaged employees a foothold to become strong leaders in their organizations.

The book is a distinguished continuation of Kathleen's first book called *Rules of Engagement for Communicating at Work*, because its chapters are structured along the same Character Model described earlier. The chapters in this book are rich with examples, and offer a handy toolbox of questions to ask and acronyms to use. Written in the same quick-read style as her first book, this work makes intuitive sense. The text draws from years of experience and is often supported by referenced research publications that help bring perspective and that add a tone of seriousness – we can make a difference. Happy reading!

Carina Fiedeldey-Van Dijk, PhD
ePsy Consultancy, Toronto

Open Letter to Leaders

Dear Leader,

This book will prove that Authentic, Engaging Leaders create Engaged Employees who produce Superior Results, and that Character (Inside Out Development) is the foundation of Authentic, Engaging Leadership.

The concepts in this book are based on my years of experience, supported by solid research. Like any good leader, however, you will draw your own conclusions. This journey is yours.

Two pivotal realizations have inspired this book.

The first is personal, though I suspect not unique. Just like many of you, I have endeavored to communicate effectively, which really means to work with people harmoniously and collaboratively. I have often felt confused regarding the rules of communication, which involve human behavior on many levels.

I have seen people labeled, criticized and excluded based not only on poor communication but also on misunderstandings, vague stories and personal agendas. Through my journey to understand the meaning of true respect and the nature of healthy relationships, one thing has become abundantly clear to me: Effective communication is by no means automatic. It requires intention and discipline – it takes work, in more ways than one.

In the workplace I observed that people can have a misunderstanding or difference of opinion, discuss it calmly, and reach a mutually acceptable outcome and achieve a deeper understanding of each other, with no hard feelings. I also witnessed an appreciation for differences between people and the choices they made. The principles of effective interaction started to emerge.

My early sense of confusion has evolved into a sense of gratitude and purpose. What I have focused on learning (and continue to learn) has been shared with many in the workplace. My objective in writing this book is to further clarify the *rules of engagement at work* and to offer tools that help leaders decrease conflict and increase collaboration, to get more meaning out of their work – and to lead by engagement.

Working with leaders is the second source of my inspiration. While I believe that the absolute majority of people want to do the right thing, I know that determining the right course of action can be as perplexing as it is challenging. The Character Model in this book has been crucial in helping me and others make choices that are intentional, conscious, and engaging.

My work history has given me the advantage of experiencing several perspectives. I started my career as an hourly employee and soon became a young manager. Later, I taught management skills in the college and university setting, and went on to become a training manager with a focus on bringing the best resources I could find, to promote healthy, productive communication in the workforce.

Over the years I have added a master's degree and spent a significant amount of time learning and exploring a variety of concepts related to communication. For the last fifteen years, I have had the enormous privilege of being an independent corporate trainer and coach to thousands of leaders.

My work has taken me from Istanbul to Honolulu, from factories in the southern United States to the skyscrapers of New York City, from the Caribbean to the oil rush fields of Northern Alberta. I have spent time with leaders in organizations on both the east and west coasts of North America and many tiny towns in between. Learning and then working in French has been like adding another dimension to my vision and allowed me the extraordinary benefit of working in many parts of Québec and France.

In my formal training to become a corporate coach I have had "classmates" from all over the world: Japan, Russia, Korea, Australia, and the British Isles. Although from different countries, we all shared the same challenge: how to create the clarity and tools to do the right thing, to treat people in an engaging way; and how to make sure that the focus of our communication was not on fluency or eloquence, but on decency, honesty, mutual regard, and fairness – in short, the right intention.

Here is one of the key things that I learned – and it is the heart of the matter: We bring who we are to the workplace; we bring our minds, hearts, backs, and our hands – our entire selves. And we only commit, truly commit, when we *feel* properly treated.

"We pay them so they will do it" just doesn't work in today's workplace, if indeed it ever did. People may spend their entire day working for a paycheck, but without something more than money to drive them, they will not likely be engaged. This book is about treating your team members well so they will want to commit and engage in your workplace.

However, there is a lot involved in treating people well. You must treat *yourself* well, have the right *systems* in place, and know what it means to treat other people well. You must possess the skills to align your behavior with your intention to engage.

Aligning your behavior with your intention can be difficult, as you may have to make choices some people will not like. But, as you will see, engagement isn't always about being popular. Being an engaging leader is about doing the right thing.

You can create your leadership legacy by choice or by default. Being a corporate coach has taught me that when leaders are asked the right questions – about their beliefs, purpose, thoughts and feelings and they take the time to reflect on their answers – they make good choices.

That is where character comes into it. Your character is you. When you make choices from the inside out, you are doing so according to your authentic character. The element of self-awareness is an important distinction here, as engaging leaders make choices deliberately.

Good choices require good tools, information and strategies, as well as reflection. The challenge for many leaders is that their busy day-to-day lives allow too little room for reflection and direction as to *how* they can better engage their teams.

This book contains the tools utilized by thousands of leaders to become more engaging leaders. Our Character Model and Engagement Strategies can help you build your authentic character into your leadership and into your organization.

My hope is that you reflect upon the ideas presented here and choose your legacy. The Character Model, which has been graphically enhanced in this book to reflect the multi-dimensional nature of character, will assist you in understanding yourself, your organization, and your legacy; and the Engagement Strategies form a workable plan of action for you to turn your choice into reality. It all hinges on you, your character.

As you will see throughout the book, we have defined character with a model in which intentions, thoughts, feelings, and behavior (words and actions) all work together in an interdependent fashion. So powerful is this model that we have designed it right into the structure of each chapter: intention (introduction), thoughts and feelings (the main body), and behavior (application).

This was done not only to illustrate how character can apply to all workplace endeavors, but also to make your reading experience more enjoyable.

Everyone is a leader in their own life, and in their own work. That was the premise in my first book, *Rules of Engagement for Communicating at Work*. In this book we are defining a leader as any person who is responsible for the contribution of others.

So, if that is you and you want to feel fully engaged and consequently fully engage the people who work with you, I sincerely hope you enjoy this journey.

Best wishes,
Kathleen

Character

The intention of Character – The Core is to shine a spotlight to the engagement crisis in the workplace, the impact of this state and a character based solution.

We will present the belief that inside out, character based leadership is the authentic, sustainable method of attracting retaining, and energizing talented employees who will make your organization a success.

Character–The Core

*To put the world right in order, we must first put the nation in order;
to put the nation in order, we must put our family in order; to put our
family in order, we must first cultivate our personal life; we must set our
hearts right.*

Confucius

There is something wrong in the workplace. You likely have felt the crush of
crises too often and have wondered *why*. The majority of people are less than
fully engaged at work; they are not completely committed to what they are
doing, and we need employee commitment for a variety of reasons.

Engagement can attract the best employees, keep them around, and inspire
them to do their best for themselves and for your organization. Engagement
is a win-win outcome that will ultimately help us maintain our high standard
of living.

A lack of engagement may seem baffling in a well-educated, prosperous
society. We should have no reason to feel anything but the rush of optimism
and clarity of purpose, right? The issue of engagement cannot be addressed
by saying we've got it good. Our prosperity is by no means guaranteed to
last, and while some people are engaged, many others drag themselves to
work and buy lottery tickets.

Years of experience as a manager and coach has given me insight as to why
so many people aren't engaged. The simple answer is that there is a lack of
trust in many leaders and therefore organizations.

The immediate issue for you, as the leader, is how to put your workplace
in order by building character and engaging your team. The consequences
of a poorly performing team are lost money, time, and opportunities, not to
mention the damage to your sense of well-being when you devote your day
to an environment fraught with a feeling of futility.

This book will explore our workplace crisis and how you can build a highly engaged culture through character–yours and that of your team members. Fortunately there is research to substantiate my observations and your gut feelings about the level of disengagement in the workplace.

Let's start with the numbers.

Gauging Our Engagement

A number of significant studies have revealed alarming data about engagement, or the lack thereof. Perhaps the most comprehensive and exciting of these is the Towers Perrin Global Workforce Study (2005). Conducted in 16 countries, the study found that of roughly 86,000 employees (median age 37, mostly managers, specialists or salaried staff), the vast majority are less than fully engaged.

In Canada as many are disengaged as are highly engaged, both at 17 percent. The findings in the United States aren't much better, with 16 percent disengaged and 21 percent highly engaged.[1]

Highly engaged employees freely give the extra effort, but disengaged employees might as well not even show up to work. Having been soured by negative experiences or their value systems, they have no respect for their organizations.

So, where do the rest fall? The largest segment, in almost every country, is that of "moderately engaged" employees. Moderate. Let the word tumble off your tongue. Do you want to hang your hopes on *moderate*? Middle of the road may work for politics and steeped tea, but in the business of engagement, moderate results are not enough.

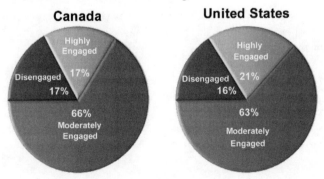

"In Canada, as many are disengaged as are highly engaged, both at 17 percent."

What's on the Bottom Line?

Our standard of living is based, in large part, on the performance of our organizations. Overwhelmingly, studies show that high engagement levels positively impact productivity and costs, whereas disengagement negatively impacts the bottom line.

The Towers Perrin Global Workforce Study found that of engaged employees, 84 percent feel they can improve quality, 68 percent feel they can decrease costs, and 71 percent feel that they can enhance customer service. The numbers in each of these three categories get worse as engagement decreases. Of moderately engaged employees, 62 percent feel they can improve quality, 42 percent feel they can decrease costs, and 50 percent feel they can enhance customer service. Finally, for disengaged employees, the results were 31 percent, 19 percent, and 27 percent, respectively.[2]

Here's a second look:

	Highly Engaged Employees	Moderately Engaged Employees	Disengaged Employees
Feel they can improve quality	84%	62%	31%
Feel they can decrease costs	68%	42%	19%
Feel they can enhance customer service	71%	50%	27%

It would be unfair not to let some other big studies join in on the conversation. So let's keep going.

In 2004, Hewitt Associates conducted a study of companies with double-digit growth (DDG) and those with only single-digit growth (SDG). The results were telling. Not only do DDG companies have more engaged leaders but they also enjoy 39 percent more engaged employees, who love their work, and 45 percent fewer disengaged employees.[3]

Finally, Watson Wyatt Worldwide conducted a U.S. study in 2006/2007 which put the productivity value of the top 25 percent of engaged employees at $276,000 in revenue per employee. The same measure for the bottom 25 percent of disengaged employees came in at just $236,000. That's a difference of $40,000 per employee.[4]

Do the math for your own department or organization. What's on your bottom line? The difference between high engagement levels versus low engagement levels is hardly chump change; and then there is the employee retention issue, which we will look at later.

Though numbers, methodologies, and definitions differ from study to study, all the results point to one troubling conclusion: Much is at stake and not enough of us are doing what we can to perform at our best, for our companies and for ourselves.

Speaking of definitions, just what is employee engagement? Quite simply, our definition of **Employee Engagement** is the readiness, willingness, and ability of your team members to improve their performance and thereby achieve sustainable success for your organization.

Every time this issue has been raised in one of our seminars, participants have expressed the heavy truth that many people in their organization are working without enthusiasm, commitment, or adequate contribution–what might be characterized as being on autopilot. Even worse, some people are actively disengaged; that is, they are hurting, hindering, or otherwise undermining the efforts of engaged employees.

Consider your own workplace. Who is on your front line, representing your team, your products–your brand? Most people want to do their best, to make a difference in their daily lives. At the very least, enlightened self-interest should impel people to look alive on the job. Clearly the workplace is not working as well as it could be. The question is, why not?

The Changing Workplace and Constant Stress

With few exceptions, today's workplace is becoming more and more stressful. A Buffet Taylor National Wellness study in 2000, conducted across 400 companies, found that stress was a major workplace health risk.[5] This is not surprising, as it's a competitive world, after all, to paraphrase a line from the classic song by Depeche Mode.[6]

The challenge of competing in a global workplace and the accelerating pace of work can turn a workplace emotionally toxic, and the fumes are both unpleasant and expensive.

Depression costs the United States between $30 billion and $44 billion annually, resulting in 200 million lost work days each year[7]; and costs Canada roughly $1 billion per year.[8]

You have probably seen the symptoms in your own organization: high number of sick days, exceptionally elevated turnover, low morale, increased stress leave, poor reputation as a preferred employer, "presenteeism" and people looking for a job while on the job. This is hardly a picture of full employee engagement.

Maybe a lack of focus is the problem. Ask yourself why people are not really present at work, in body or in spirit.

A joint study involving Ipsos-Reid, WarrenShepell, and the Human Resources Professionals Association of Ontario (HRPAO), in 2004, found the top three contributors to absenteeism and health costs were depression, anxiety and other mental health disorders (66 percent); stress (60 percent); and relationship with supervisor/manager (44 percent).[9]

That last point above is by no means last in significance. Your job title may be that of manager, supervisor, or director, but your true role is that of leader. Leadership is more than just a role, it's a process. When the process isn't working, engagement drops, and the stress of your employees can become your stress.

A study by WarrenShepell found that managers and supervisors account for 18 percent to 37 percent (depending on the industry) of all Employee Assistance Program (EAP) accesses, whereas the study's average manager-to-direct report ratio was 1:10, or 10 percent.[10]

Managers are shouldering a disproportionate amount of stress.

REALITY BITES

Beleaguered by Leadership: Patricia's Story

Patricia is a leader and hates being one. An energetic twenty-eight year old, she began working for a successful high-tech firm seven years ago. Having studied math and science, Patricia enjoys creating and getting things done with a hands-on approach. However, when her leader asked her to become a team leader two years ago, she insisted she wasn't leadership material.

Responsible and hardworking, she took on the role.

When she came to realize that she had no idea how to deal with the various work formats – cooperative students, full-time people, people on contract working virtually in other countries, temporary workers and part-time employees, the many older employees–Patricia started treating her team badly, losing her temper, perceiving her challenges as a poor work ethic on their part.

Patricia is considering quitting the company; she sees it as her only solution. When this bright and talented young woman attended an emotional intelligence workshop, she was at her wit's end. We eventually helped Patricia, but her difficulties illustrate just one set of challenges facing young leaders today. We will return to Patricia later.

Clearly, managers are feeling the strain. If this sounds familiar, you need to change the way you understand and approach your role. So where do you look first? Start with a picture of the authentically engaging leader.

The Definition of Leadership by Engagement

Leadership by Engagement encompasses your readiness, willingness, and ability to leverage all facets of your authentic character in order to attract, retain, and energize employees that will achieve sustainable success for your organization.

The Look of Leadership by Engagement

Being a leader is about more than tracking skill sets and vacation days. As a leader, your goal is to powerfully engage the greatest number of your employees, so that they in turn can create and realize aggressive goals and targets, share information in all directions, and treat all people in their sphere with courtesy and civility. The desired and ultimate outcome of engagement is fewer wasted days, better results for all, and a reputation based on the reality that it is genuinely fun to work in your organization.

And if you have any doubts about the potential effect you have on the people around you, lay them to rest now. Like it or not, you can play a central and emotional role in the work lives of your employees.

The Feel of Leadership by Engagement

Anyone who has ever seen a movie about football or about a group of townsfolk beset by a seemingly insurmountable challenge will recall the big emotional speech the chief makes to rally people and gain resolve.

Such scenes, though scripted, are imitating life and reflecting a truth we know deep down: leaders lead by stirring our emotions and energizing us to do our best for ourselves and for our team.

Daniel Goleman, author of *Emotional Intelligence*, wrote in his follow-up book, *Primal Leadership: Learning to Lead with Emotional Intelligence*, that it is leaders who have the greatest power to move people emotionally; that if people are excited and passionate about their work, their "performance can soar." Conversely, if people's emotions spiral down into negativity, anxiety, and bitterness, they will be "thrown off stride," and their performance will suffer.[11]

Further evidence exists as to the importance of managers. A study by BlessingWhite, entitled *Employee Engagement Report 2006*, which was conducted across three continents including North America, found that because managers can make connections between the career ambitions of team members and the goals and objectives of the organization, they are uniquely positioned to increase employee engagement.[12]

Goleman also wrote that leaders serve a primordial emotional role within any team.[13] Since time immemorial we have looked to leaders for clarity in an uncertain, dangerous, and ever-changing world.

Today, the job of the leader has never been more complex. Yes, the workplace has changed and continues to change, along with the people who come to work.

The Challenge of the Changing Workforce

Diversity is healthy for an organization when employees are engaged and working together, but it is just the opposite when they aren't. Consider our current labour pool. It is comprised of the following:

- Young people who have seen adults downsized, restructured and scrambling to ensure cash flow in their later working years.
- Baby boomers who are working until pensions commence.
- "Cash Flow versus a Career." Individuals who have given up on corporate careers and accept jobs below their capacity.
- People who have retired with a pension and choose to continue to work and contribute.
- Newcomers who want to integrate into the workplace and are anxious to learn norms and standards of their new environments.
- Cynics of all ages who have been disappointed by deceitful, greedy behavior on the part of individuals and organizations.
- Temporary workers who move from job to job and have no obvious reason to commit themselves to the organizations where they are "placed."
- People who are choosing alternative working lives–virtual companies, home-office arrangements, or on the road but connected by blackberries and cell phones.

The ethnic diversity of the workplace alone would warrant a separate book. Suffice to say, the advantage of having people of varying cultures and perspectives in your organization can be offset by their lack of common ground.

The ground is always shifting. The worldwide temporary placement industry takes in billions of dollars per year, placing hundreds of thousands of workers globally. However, if you have ever worked for one you will know the score. Often temping is a means to an end for young people and freelancers, a way to make some money without making a big commitment, possibly a way to get a foot in the door. Attempts to engage people in this group may prove difficult as many of them will not be in the same place for more than a few weeks or months.

Conversely, there are temporary employees recruited from other countries who may be totally dedicated to your organization, who face other stresses related to this unusual situation. This circumstance requires surveillance and strong communication.

Then there are employees who are someplace else all the time. In the past fifteen years we have seen the creation of a culture of "virtual" employees. Though "out of office" does not necessary mean out of passion, staff who work independently present a particular challenge: How do you convey organizational culture and expectations with the same clarity and enthusiasm you impart with the office team you see every day?

It's not hard to see why young managers today are stressed out. Add to this the ever pressing bottom line and you have a workforce and workplace that would be unrecognizable to our grandparents.

Finally, we would be remiss if we didn't look at the various generations at work.

The Challenge of the Ages

Boom, boom, boom went the workforce! Baby boomers started working when today's younger managers were in diapers, and they will continue to be with us in one way or another for some time to come. In Canada, there will be twice as many seniors as children by 2031.[14] In the United States, 40 percent of the workforce will be retirement age by 2010, which will leave a shortfall of 10 million workers between the ages of 25 and 44.[15] At least in Canada the mandatory retirement age is no longer 65. Of course, this means many boomers will choose to keep working.

The challenge here is two-fold. A shortage of middle-aged workers means your organization must appeal to bright, restless, young people in order to survive, whereas an abundance of boomers with busy lives and plenty of experience means you will need to appeal to their desire for flexibility, independence, and respect.

REALITY BITES

Older, Wiser, and Trapped: Bruce's Story

Bruce started with a manufacturing company directly out of college. It was his first full-time job, so he worked hard, was totally loyal to the company, and enjoyed the payoff of being steadily promoted through his thirty-four year tenure.

As the company was part of a specialized industry, they sent Bruce on many internal and external training programs. In time, his technical prowess became deep and broad, and he developed a vast network of respected colleagues, who in turn valued and respected his abilities. It would be safe to say the Bruce felt satisfied and engaged.

Then, five years ago, the company was sold, to new owners who knew little about the industry and saw only a cash rich opportunity. Senior leadership was replaced by cronies of the new owners.

As a senior middle manager, Bruce now reports to a new leader from the financial sector, a man who places no value on his technical skills or his vast knowledge of the industry.

Bruce often feels humiliated and frustrated; he feels trapped. He has stock options in this company and wants to protect his retirement income, and is loath to leave. At fifty-six years old he feels old, yet not ready financially and emotionally to retire. So, he hesitates to start interviewing with other companies, fearing his skills and network limit him to one industry. He is currently waiting it out to see if the company will be sold again. Perhaps new owners would value and respect him.

Bruce's story is not uncommon, unfortunately. As a leader, you must figure out how to keep people like Bruce engaged.

Let's take a look at another boomer, a talented woman who found her path to engagement–through flowers and flexibility.

Marsha's Fresh Arrangement

Marsha taught public school for thirty-four years and loved it. However, in her last years as a teacher, desiring change, she took a course in flower arranging. When she retired this year at fifty-four years old, Marsha found a job in the flower shop of a local grocery store, where she now works anywhere from fifteen to thirty-five hours per week. She is truly enjoying it, and it has everything to do with lifestyle.

"No preparation, when I leave the store, the work stays there. Secondly, I am caring for my aging Mom and still have two children at home. My boss is very flexible and allows me as much time off as I require. There are a few people retired like me and as long as we cover the shifts, everyone is happy. Finally, this work, even though it is much less money than I made as a teacher, provides some cash and a place to go and people to be around on a regular basis. Right now I am looking forward to our store Christmas party."

The Way of All Fresh Arrangements

Though the workforce is a complex and ever-changing mixture of boomers, Generation Xers and Y's, temporary workers, immigrants, and virtual workers, each and every one of your team members presents you with the same challenge: how not to lose them before you engage them!

Everyone seeks options, and some people choose to leave.

To Mention Retention

Generally speaking, people value mobility. In a free economy people will come and go of their own volition (or sometimes escorted to the front door). However, too much turnover is bad for business when employees leave without ever maximizing their contribution to the organization.

Some estimates put the cost of turnover at 150 percent of the employee's salary, or as much as 250 percent for managers and sales staff.[16] When you consider the cost of orientation, training, mistakes, lost productivity, jittery customers, resistance by existing employees, and the negative reputation "on the street," the full cost of turnover may be immeasurable. It is to be minimized.

Add to the above the loss of experience when senior employees are lost or disengaged and you also have a corresponding loss of experience and culture to go with your lost dollars. We saw this earlier in Bruce's story.

Conversely, organizations known for high engagement levels perpetuate their success by attracting the best candidates, but even before you can gain a stellar reputation you first have to achieve great results with the people around you. As a leader, you must determine how best to retain your team members long enough to achieve higher engagement levels.

Ask yourself why people are at work in the first place, and why they decide to leave. We already know about the potentially powerful relationship between you and your team members. Let's take another look at the numbers.

A survey by Ipsos-Reid found that the top two considerations when looking for work are money (39 percent) and a positive work environment (33 percent).[17] So what makes for positive work environment?

According to Towers Perrin, the top three drivers of retention are 1) the organization retains the right people, 2) the organization makes the right people decisions, and 3) the manager understands how to motivate.[18]

We're getting closer to the heart of it.

BlessingWhite found that strong manager-employee relationships are crucial to employee engagement and retention. Furthermore, leaders who reveal a bit about themselves will cultivate trust in their team members; and leaders who get to know their team members will be better able to lead them to achievements that are personally meaningful and valuable to the organization.[19]

Finally, Sirota Survey Intelligence reveals that employees who feel their managers **do not respect them** are three times more likely to leave their places of work in the next two years.[20]

NO CONTEST

Of course, those of you who have spent some years in the workplace may know that people who leave their jobs will not always enter a robust economy full of opportunities. What about during downturns, such as the current global economic crisis? If respect is crucial in good times, it is even more so during ones that will challenge your organization to the core. While the economy may be "free," it isn't always easy or forgiving. So what is necessary to ensure your place in the market?

Superior engagement is always the way to ensure you and your team are best prepared to deal with external realities as well as internal fears. Cutting costs during dire times won't address the fundamental issue here. In fact, it will likely disengage your team. To keep your people highly engaged, you must seize the one clear opportunity that is always available to leaders: to cultivate trust by communicating with your employees as clearly and honestly as possible, to encourage high performance and results. Getting the best from your people will steer your organization away from the rocks of failure as much as it will make it soar.

"Of course, knowing that work is about people is the easy part. Doing something about it is another matter entirely. Whether you are new to your role as a leader or have been at it a while, you will always be faced with the same challenge: how to develop engaging working relationships.

"The good news is that we know what you can do about it. You first have to *feel* it."

Enter the Leadership Engagement Behaviors: The Caring of Character

Never apologize for showing feeling. When you do so, you apologize for the truth.

Benjamin Disraeli

After years of field work and research, my associates and I have learned what makes an engaging, character-driven leader. We have learned what behaviors bring people on board and inspire them to do their best.

Remarkably, the Towers Perrin Workforce study reveals that the top engagement driver is the same for Canada as it is for the United States. Whatever their differences, the two countries share a very simple truth about working life: Employees want their leaders to demonstrate "interest in employee well-being."[21]

Yes, you have to care about your team members, in other words. That's right – care. Think about it. How can you expect employees to care about the performance and well-being of your organization when you don't show them the same consideration?

According to the Ivey Business Journal, perks alone will not inspire top performance in workers if a gap exists between the leader and the team. Rather, leaders who value their employees will get the best from them. Employee engagement is a direct indication of how they feel about their boss.[22]

Caring is about valuing your employees, about cultivating trust. It's about you choosing to engage your team members, for the benefit of individual employees and your organization. Character is about this process, as we will see very shortly. Caring and character go together, but what does this mean in terms of specific leadership behaviors?

Without further ado, if you want to lead your team to engagement and thereby get the best from them, do the following:

The Leadership Engagement Behaviors	
1.	Treat people in a consistently civil manner.
2.	Tell the truth.
3.	Listen openly with empathy.
4.	Conduct yourself in an ethical manner.
5.	Create an atmosphere of camaraderie.
6.	Provide autonomy to make decisions.
7.	Articulate clear, measurable, achievable performance expectations.
8.	Recognize contributions frequently, specifically and personally.
9.	Address performance gaps in a timely, private, problem solving manner.
10.	Provide opportunities for people to find challenge and significance in their work.
11.	Ensure training and learning opportunities are available.
12.	Provide proper tools and resources.

By using the **Leadership Engagement Behaviors,** you will set in motion a process of communication and action that will demonstrate your respect and caring and will also heighten the engagement level in your team. Leading by Engagement is about more than your job title or the tactics you use to get yourself ahead. It is about intentionally cultivating and maintaining a healthy working environment in order to achieve shared goals. It is about appealing to the hearts and the minds of your team. Ultimately, it is about gaining trust. Not surprisingly, therefore, the above behaviors are connected to something deeper than the jumbo double-double coffees that get some people going in the morning.

REALITY BITES

Why Pure Behavior Training Is Suspect

"Communication Skills" training is big business. And the training, the "skill development", is typically focused on changing behavior. I should know, because I spent years conducting training programs all over North

America. Often a participant would approach me during a break or lunch hour and say something like, "I have taken many of these courses. I want to know how to say the right thing in the right way when it counts." Clearly, a fundamental aspect of who we are wasn't being addressed by communication skills training programs.

I realized that communication skills would work if treated only as an add-on; that to be a truly effective and engaging leader required a more holistic behavioral approach.

What was the missing connection?

The Character Connection

If history is a record of character meeting circumstance, to paraphrase Donald G. Creighton, a Canadian historian, what will people remember about your character and how you handled your circumstances? And what, or who, determines your ability to lead through your character?

We have all heard the expression that leaders are born and not made, and vice versa. My experience has shown me that true leaders make themselves. This is not to dismiss the fact that some people are born with magnetic and persuasive qualities. But the **Leadership Engagement Behaviors** speak to how leaders at every level channel organizational values by applying them to everyday situations, and these behaviors speak to how we decide to treat each other at work–the character of our organization.

Our work is firmly founded on the concept of character for good reason. Since 1993, we have worked directly with leaders at every level, and have seen that true change starts from the inside and happens in an intentional, focused manner. Sending people on a course or two in "communication skills" is a superficial and short-sighted approach, one which may provide empty rhetoric without real change.

Think about how any meaningful change has happened in your life. Whether you quit smoking, lost weight, chose a career, or got married, chances are you drew from deep within yourself. The same applies to leadership by engagement. The insight, decision, planning and discipline must come from you, from your will, from your character. To become an engaging leader, you must proactively develop the character of your organization, your team, and yourself.

Character: What Does It Take To Engage?

I recognized the immensity of the challenge of this question which had sparked my own journey to understand and practice assertive, healthy, constructive communication. What I learned is that honest, authentic communication is not simple and requires every element of us, our entire being–our character.

Character guides us from the inside out and spreads to all aspects of our lives. A person of healthy character thinks carefully about what she is trying to achieve and channels all her being into accomplishing the goal in a way that respects her own needs and the needs of others.

Easier said than done, you might argue. Not only are circumstances rarely ideal, but human dynamics are infinitely complex. What sets true leaders apart is that they consciously try to understand themselves and others as well. Not to be confused with idle navel gazing, purposeful self-assessment is a healthy pursuit that can maximize our potential and behavior more effectively.

My experiences have shown that achieving objectives requires that I "think" about my feelings and my reactions to various situations, so that I can understand my decisions and actions. Knowing the layers of oneself is a necessary step in self-management and in becoming an engaging leader. How can you lead others if you cannot lead yourself?

Character: A Model of Leadership

What is at the core of the **Leadership Engagement Behaviors?**

Many of us are aware of the two types of intelligence we hope for in a leader: cognitive and emotional. However, these faculties alone will not explain behavior. At the core of the mind is what psychologists call *conation,* more commonly understood as the mental processes involved in striving–motivation, desire, volition, and resolve.[23] When conation is viewed in a particular context, we call it intention, and it's a powerful starting place, for it's all of our intentions, working in concert with self-discipline, that drive us to achieve our goals.

To achieve the results we intend, however, we must see our plans through the often bumpy terrain of thoughts and emotions that can be difficult to manage, never mind master, without a practical structure to help us make the right choices.

Our **Character Model** is a layered framework that addresses this and other fundamental questions and has helped me and my clients achieve the results we want.

Your Character at Work

Character is the result of two things: mental attitude and the way we spend our time.

Elbert Hubbard

You are your character and your character is you. In order to behave as you choose, rather than just reacting, you must work from the inside out to illuminate, strengthen and align your words and actions. The layers of character are interwoven, interactive and interdependent. How well these elements work together will depend on who you are as a leader.

Character Leadership is your readiness, willingness, and ability to master your thoughts, feelings, and leadership behaviors in order to align them with your intention to lead by engagement.

Here is a graphic depiction of character, applied to you as a leader in your workplace.

Your Character

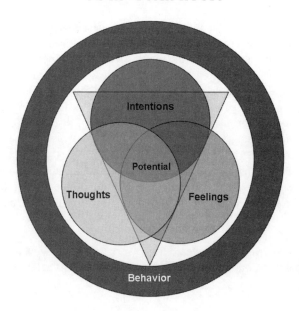

Intentions (Conation: What Motivates You)

Your intentions encompass your purpose, beliefs, and goals as a leader.

Purpose: What leadership legacy do you wish to leave? What motivates you? What attitude do you bring to this job?

Beliefs: What you believe about leadership, engagement, communication, other people and yourself as defined by your principles and values.

- Principles–what you believe to be true and important.
- Values–your guidelines regarding how to treat yourself, your organization and others.

Goals: In a more situational fashion, your priorities and objectives.

- Priorities–what is most urgent, most important?
- Objectives–what you are trying to achieve at any given point in time, in one conversation or interaction?

Your decision to practice the **Leadership Engagement Behaviors** is made at the intention level, when you determine what you believe to be right and valuable to you, your team and your organization. Having the *discipline* to follow through on your intentions is crucial: No plan will work without it, so it should be the linchpin of your internal process.

Thoughts (How You Think – Messages from Your Mind)

This is your thinking process–your ability to reason, evaluate, and solve problems. However, thinking is not just about how skillfully you handle technical problems. In order to behave in a manner that supports all aspects of your character (intentions, feelings, and behavior) and produce powerful, constructive results, awareness of your thinking process is essential.

Feelings (Cues from Your Body/Emotions)

This is about knowing in a different way–being able to "know" on an emotional level.

Sometimes you just know. Sometimes your body is talking to you. At some point, you've probably experienced tension in the shoulders, clenched teeth or a knotted stomach. Such powerful sensations allow you to feel your emotions, providing information that can help you understand yourself, what is happening to you and to others around you.

Feelings play a significant role in leadership, for empathy and understanding are impossible without them. Your ability to master your emotions, particularly during times of stress, will help you engage the people on your team.

Behavior (The Manifestation of Intentions, Thoughts and Feelings)

While some of your school teachers may have told you good behavior is about being quiet in class, leadership behavior in the **Character Model** describes the skills you employ to communicate with others; what you say and how you say it; the words, tone, and body language you use to say it. In short, it's the words and actions you choose. Behaving to authentically engage others requires that you proactively align your words and actions with your intentions, thoughts, and feelings.

When you are leading through your authentic character, the outer ring of your **Character Model** will be your unique expression of the **Leadership Engagement Behaviors.**

This is your potential.

Your Character Potential

Your greatest character potential lies in your ability to align and integrate your intentions, thoughts, feelings, and behaviors, to achieve the best results possible as you build and lead your team. However, marshalling your character requires self-control, both proactively and reactively speaking.

You will note the use of the word *proactive* throughout this book. Although leading according to one's character requires intentionality and deliberation, there are times when you will find yourself having to react to unforeseen situations and unanticipated emotions.

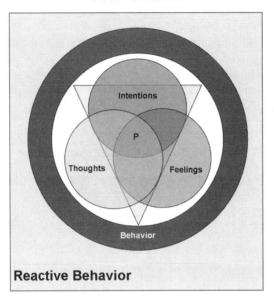

Reactive or Proactive Your Choice

Reactive Behavior

Later we will look at how to gain self-mastery, but for now, take a look at the center of the **Character Model.** You will see a *large triangle*. This figure is the basis for a practical tool we will explore in chapter three, which can help you align all the aspects of your character by practicing self-control.

Speaking of self…

Personality: Forever Jung? Just Be Yourself

By now you may be asking yourself where personality fits into all of this. The short answer is, everywhere. While the **Character Model** provides us with a structure to help us explain and proactively manage our behavior, personality works as an integral and innate aspect of ourselves, which influences the outward expression of our entire character.

Since antiquity people have been described as having natural gifts, talents, styles, and preferences. Our oldest descriptions date back to the Greek philosopher Empedocles, who promulgated the notion of temperaments reflecting the elements of air, water, earth, and fire.

In the modern era we saw the rise and evolution of psychology, and the development of such tools as the Myers-Briggs Type Indicator® (MBTI), based on the science of psychologist Carl Jung. A giant in the field of self-determination, Jung described personality as "the affirmation of all that constitutes an individual."[24] Essentially, personality is your natural gifts and predispositions.

Though the MBTI can be used to understand people as innately introverted or extraverted, analytical or intuitive and so on, the debate continues as to how much of human personality is inborn and how much is learned.

In the **Character Model** there is no debate: You have a choice regarding how you intend to behave and the tools you use to manage your thoughts and feelings in order to act in alignment with your intentions. Those of you who fear this approach will diminish individuality will find that just the opposite is true; focusing on your character will reveal who you *really* are!

Change Is Going to Come

You behave a certain way as a result of your upbringing, habits and comfort level. Can you change how you behave? Yes, but it requires an inside–out, conscious commitment. Consciously decide upon your intentions, master your emotions, manage your thoughts and align your behavior.

In *Working with Emotional Intelligence,* Goleman wrote that it is indeed possible for us to change our habits at the neurological level. We learn new competencies by replacing the brain's automatic responses with new ones. When this practice is taken to its desired outcome, our old habit will no longer be our default response because a new pattern of responses will have taken the place of the old one. So, over time, we can change our thoughts, our actions, and our performance.[25]

In short, we can enhance our character.

This is great news! Our character is determined by how the layers of ourselves work together. Our character is judged by how we present ourselves to the world. Our character is remembered for the results we achieve, and you wouldn't be reading this book if you weren't interested in results.

Recap of Thoughts

In this chapter, we have looked at data and findings which support what we all observe as a lack of engagement in the workplace. We have read stories and considered what thinkers of yesteryear said about character. Also, we have seen there is a connection between character and engagement behavior, and a structure to guide us.

The **Character Model** provides the core for **Leadership Engagement Behaviors.** The focus on character creates authentic, strong, sustainable positive behaviors which are required to truly engage your team.

Putting It into Words and Actions

Theory alone will not result in engagement through authentic character leadership, unless you know how the concepts we've discussed in this chapter can be used to improve your workplace. Below are four main practical steps you can take to begin on the path to engagement.

Start by considering your organization.

1. Determining the Current State of Engagement

Start to gather some data in order to establish a benchmark in your organization or department:

- How difficult is it to attract the right people?
- What is the employee turnover rate?
- Why are people really leaving? Consider asking an objective person to conduct exit reviews and gather good data.
- What is your employee turnover cost?
- What is your rate of absenteeism or perfect days (everyone present)?
- Are there incidents of stress leave?
- What is the cost of your organization's disability premiums?
- What do your customer satisfaction surveys indicate?
- What are the results from your quality measurements revealing?

- What is your Employee Assistance Plan usage? (The more your staff are proactively dealing with issues and concerns, the better).
- How are you assessing morale?
- What is the level of morale?

You first have to understand what isn't working in your organization before you can find what will work.

Next determine if you behavior is working to engage your team as it should.

2. The Leadership Engagement Behaviors

How well do you practice the **Leadership Engagement Behaviors?**

To help you assess just how well you are currently engaging your team, we invite you to take our *Are You Engaged* quiz at:

www.centreforcharacterleadership.com/engagequiz.com

You will have an opportunity to take a more formal assessment later in the book. For now, however, the score you receive by doing the above test will give you an idea of how much work you need to do to become a fully, authentically engaging leader.

3. Care about the Person – Judge the Behavior

Next time you find yourself not liking someone, see if you can separate the person and their behavior. Find a way to want the best for the person, to be committed to their success, and at the same time identify the workplace behaviors that are inappropriate.

In order to engage people we must care for them. People know when we don't like them. Engaging leaders focus on improving behavior, not condemning people. Build your team – attract, retain, and energize them – don't tear them down. This is character leadership.

4. Character Concept

- Start to notice how you are applying the **Character Model** concepts.
- Observe yourself in significant conversations.
- How clear is your intention before entering into a significant conversation?
- Do you notice your feelings?
- How do you manage them? Ignore? Factor in your intuitive insights?
- Do you behave in alignment with your intentions or does something ambush you?
- When are you in "reactive" mode?
- How well is this serving you in creating a leadership legacy?
- What are you learning about yourself?

Learning–about yourself and about your team–is what authentic character leadership is all about.

In the coming chapters we will examine in greater detail how our **Character Model** can be used to help you behave authentically and engagingly in specific situations. We will look at **Five Strategies** for Engagement: Clarify the Culture, Know Your Character, Respect Yourself, Respect Others, and Harness Conflict. The development of these five chapters will lead us to the final chapter–Build Trust.

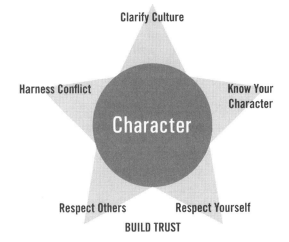

Strategies for Engagement

Clarify the Culture will help you to communicate clearly and thereby achieve a team culture of engagement through character. In Know Your Character, we will look at your own character and engagement levels, so you can understand how best to lead yourself. In Respect Yourself, we will provide practical measures for keeping your balance and wits in the maelstrom of daily work life. In Respect Others, we turn our attention on your team, so that you get the greatest engagement and the best results from them. Harness Conflict will show you how to deal with bullies, but we will also see that conflict is not necessarily a bad thing, that its energy can be used to fortify character and increase engagement.

These engagement strategies will enable you to create a healthy and productive work environment in which trust, the subject of our final chapter, is the norm.

In our final chapter, Build Trust, we will return to the reason why you need to be authentic and "walk the talk" in the first place. We will show how by using the **Five Strategies** you can lead through your character to achieve the ultimate human aim of engagement–to build a culture of trust so that your organization will become known as one of character and engagement.

In our next chapter, **Clarify the Culture,** we will look at how the Character Model can be used to create an engaging culture, from the inside out.

Although this book is not a quick fix, we hope it will be a quick read. If you are ready to take on your known crises, overcome your feelings of futility and make a difference then read on.

Welcome to **Leadership by Engagement.**

CLARIFY CULTURE

Character

The intention of Clarify the Culture is to ensure that you create a foundation for engagement, so that your systems, practices and policies support your engagement efforts.

Clarify the Culture offers you the opportunity to identify and enhance the character of your organization in order to more significantly engage your team.

If you are going to attract, retain, and engage the right people, you need to create a culture in which character and engagement can flourish.

Intentional Acts of Character
Caring and Courage: Taking Engagement to a New Level

Steve was appalled. As an area manager for a large fast food chain in Calgary, Alberta, he knew he had to be decisive when he discovered that fifteen of the company's new foreign workers were living in deplorable conditions: six people to a room, missing furniture, and two-hour commutes to their work in the city.

Hired and housed through an agency, the employees had journeyed from the Philippines trusting that their lodgings would not be stressfully substandard. As for the people at the agency, they had assumed all was well. When they did learn the truth, they expected the landlords would improve the living conditions in a timely manner. For Steve, however, this was not good enough, as the workers were already feeling the strain.

Confronting the landlords, Steve firmly expressed his disapproval of the situation and dismissed their claims that they planned to see to their tenants *soon*. He found an ally in Zack, the president of the company, who wholly supported Steve's decision to find the team better housing and contacted the person at the company in charge of recruiting foreign workers to ensure changes were made to the program.

Steve acted as he did because he understands the connection between employee well-being, customer satisfaction, and position in the marketplace– and in the community. His "serve in leadership" philosophy of proactively doing the right thing is reflected in the organization's values.

Today, the foreign employees under Steve's leadership are among the best in the organization. Like Steve, they are ready, willing, and able to deliver the service they intended when they came to the company. Backed by character-aligned senior management, Steve and his team are living proof that an organizational culture of engagement through authentic character produces superior results.

Clarify the Culture

It is never too late to be what we might have been.

George Eliot

Culture exists wherever you find people, place, and purpose. This is true of any workplace, and the way in which organizational culture is created will have a profound impact on the performance of its individuals, who in turn play a part in shaping and maintaining the culture.

People feel engaged at work when our leaders not only clarify best practices and set standards, but when they also lead by example and uphold those standards.

A culture of engagement starts with the leaders. As we saw in the previous chapter, people are hardwired to scrutinize their leaders, to look to them for security, even a sense of purpose. As a leader, you may neglect your team and get a culture by default, or try to create a culture without truly understanding the nature of the people in your workplace. Both of these approaches will create confusion, turmoil, and disengagement. Your team is looking to you to clarify their culture.

Clarifying the culture means proactively, honestly and explicitly creating an organizational culture of engagement from the inside out, by applying the **Character Model**. As you will see, the **Character Model** applies to organizations as it does to individuals.

In this chapter, we talk about focusing on the intention to create a culture where leaders consistently practice the **Leadership Engagement Behaviors**, thoroughly consider what this concept means and how it works, and clearly identify and express the challenges at an emotional level, both for themselves and the people they lead. Clarifying the culture means creating conditions that will ensure the **Leadership Engagement Behaviors** are practiced by leaders in the organization.

The full power of engagement occurs when it is felt by all employees. Therefore, leaders must proactively create conditions in which trust and engagement can grow. This means clarifying the culture first for all the leaders, who in turn clarify the culture for their own teams and the entire organization.

All leaders must work together, to understand just what engagement means to them, what sort of culture they want, and how they plan to achieve it. Then they can take it to their teams.

See how the **Character Model** applies to your organization.

Organizational Character

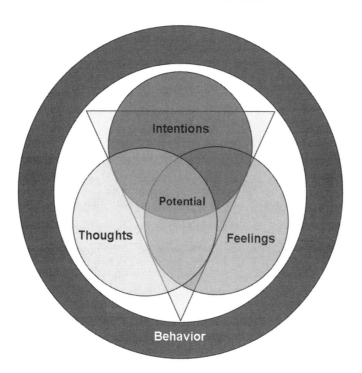

Intentions: Purpose

Engagement starts with intentions, and so does behavior. Nothing can be built around a core that is not sound–nothing that will endure, that is. This applies to your organizational culture. Here the challenge is two-fold. First, the leadership team must be on the same page. Second, they must understand what is really driving the people in the organization. In a workplace that is diverse and changing, leaders must find common ground among all employees in order to engage them.

Beliefs: Principles

Here are key questions to help your organization clarify leadership principles:

- Do we believe that it is important to engage people?
- Are the **Leadership Engagement Behaviors** applicable for our environment?
- If not, what makes sense?
- Do we, the leadership team members, treat each other in an engaging manner?
- Is it important that we are all aligned before we start working with our direct reports on engagement issues?
- Do we believe that we must understand and align our own character to apply the **Leadership Engagement Behaviors**?
- How do we ensure that each person understands his or her role in achieving departmental/organizational alignment?
- What do we believe about training leaders to create a more engaging culture?
- How do we hold leaders accountable to practice the **Leadership Engagement Behaviors**?
- Do we include the **Leadership Engagement Behaviors** as part of the leadership evaluation process?
- What do we do when leaders do not meet our standards?
- How do we measure engagement?
- What indicators do we correlate to in order to evaluate concrete results?

These questions are guidelines for understanding leadership principles with respect to engagement. But what lies beneath these specific work principles?

Beliefs: Values

The values of an organization are those beliefs held as important by all leaders and all employees; they are the core values that can lead to a culture of character when regularly expressed or demonstrated through the **Leadership Engagement Behaviors**.

Before you can expect your employees to practice engagement behaviors, however, you and the other leaders must demonstrate your organizational values by being courageous, honest, compassionate, disciplined, authentic, inclusive and fair–with each other!

A study published in the Ivey Business Journal Online found the importance of character in leaders is considerable, that the authentic leaders are those who have the self-discipline to show consistency between their values, thoughts, feelings, words, and actions. By gaining the respect of their employees, such leaders can "achieve results that transcend everyday organizational imperatives and outcomes."[1]

Agreement about the fundamental importance of character must exist among leaders before engagement can be cultivated throughout the rest of the organization.

BATTLING LEADERS

Agreement and trust in an organization can be a scarce commodity, as competition between and among managers can create silos, distance, and havoc, making it difficult for leaders to get to know one another. Also, depending on the character of the most senior leader, the others may be caught in a dance of duck and weave.

You and the other members of the Senior Leadership Team must create a culture of trust. The **Leadership Engagement Behaviors**, for the most part, work horizontally as well as vertically.

If this sounds overly ambitious, consider the following **Reality Bite**, a story about an entire community that put itself on the map because of the determination of its citizens to live according to character.

REALITY BITES

York Region–A Community Success Story

York Region is home to over 900,000 residents and 26,000 businesses. Bordering Toronto to the North, it is one of the most ethnically diverse populations in all of Canada.

Though in many other respects York Region is similar to other large suburban communities, it is marked by one very important distinction: In 2002 it became the first regional municipality to declare itself a "character community," in which attributes of character are embraced in homes, schools, businesses, and public organizations.

The leadership for this bold region-wide transformation came from two people. Donald Cousens, Markham's mayor at the time and Dr. Avis Glaze, the former associate director of education for the York District School Board. Dr. Glaze was committed to provide meaningful opportunities for dialogue and connection. Cousens' passion, dedication, and commitment to making York Region a better place to live, work and play was the driving force of his vision.

Dr. Glaze introduced the project to schools. Mayor Cousens introduced the project to government, businesses, and families. In a short period of time the Character Community Movement and Foundation was born.

Character in Business, Community, Schools, Family and Sport committees are thriving. In June 2006 the Ontario Legislature declared Ontario a "Province of Character." www.charactercommunity.com

"Character has become a movement in our community. Once an individual or an organization reflects on his or her character, it has a ripple effect. Good character is contagious and I am honored to be a part of making our world a better place to be. We can all work a little bit harder on doing and being our best." - Donald Cousens

Christine DeHaas
Former Executive Director of Character Community Foundation

The York Region Character Community is an example of large-scale success. Here the culture of character is clear and understood by people in all sectors of society–students, educators, parents, business owners, and politicians–and those involved actively perpetuate the culture.

Furthermore, the Regional Municipality was listed as one of Canada's top 100 employers in 2007 in a competition run by the publisher Mediocorp, the results of which ran in Maclean's magazine.[2]

If an entire region can establish and maintain a community in which character is the norm, certainly a company can do the same!

By creating a strong, united, aligned leadership, you will be able to make specific plans that will move you closer to creating a culture of engagement throughout the organization.

Let's return to the **Character Model** and clarify the workings of intentions.

Goals: Priorities

- What are your leadership priorities in creating a culture of engagement?
- How do you balance the requirement to produce tangible outcomes while maintaining an engaging culture?
- Who should be aware of this process?

Goals: Objectives

- How do the priorities transform into organizational objectives?
- What is the strategy?
- What is the plan?
- How will we communicate the plan? To leaders? To all team members?
- Who is responsible for what?
- How do we inspire the leadership team to embrace the self-discipline required in applying the **Character Model** and in practicing the **Leadership Engagement Behaviors**?
- How will you measure our success?
- How can you establish milestones?
- How will you celebrate?

These questions will help you focus all of the aspects of your intentions–your organizational principles and values–so that you and other leaders can develop a measurable plan to create a culture in which **Leadership Engagement Behaviors** are an everyday practice in your organization.

When it comes to considering and creating culture, there is no better place to start than the front door–new recruits.

REALITY BITES

Four Seasons: What Is Possible with Hospitality

The stellar reputation of the Four Seasons Hotel chain is known around the world. If you have ever experienced the impeccable service of a concierge at one of their hotels or resorts, you will understand why the organization is a leader in hospitality and customer service.

How does such a wonderful employee get that way? Is it the nature of the person or is it the culture of the organization? Maybe it's a bit of both; Four Seasons will not tolerate poor performance. How do they consistently get such great staff? Who comes through their doors to work there?

The "Employment" page of the Four Seasons website can shed some light on the matter:

At Four Seasons, we place a great deal of importance on assembling the best team possible. We hire motivated people, train them to perform their jobs superbly and create a working environment where they can flourish–guided by passionately held goals, beliefs and principles. Four Seasons can offer what many hospitality professionals dream of–an opportunity to build a lifelong career that has both global potential and a real sense of pride in work well done.

Four Seasons employees make the difference for our guests by creatively demonstrating our culture of service excellence. It is this culture that sets us apart from our competitors; an intangible quality that keeps our valued guests returning again and again and drives us to deliver the best service in the industry.[3]

Can your organization truthfully make such a bold claim to excellence?

As someone who plays a role in hiring, you are familiar with the stress and difficulty of putting together the best team possible. What are your hiring practices? What are your standards, for new recruits and those already in your employ? These questions underscore the importance of clarity when establishing organizational beliefs and goals.

According to the *Right Management Survey 2006*, bad hires and promotions can lead to lower morale (68 percent), lower productivity (66 percent), lost customers (54 percent), higher training costs (51 percent), and higher recruiting costs (44 percent).[4]

Add to the above the costs of employee turnover, and we have further evidence that a poorly performing team can have an impact on the bottom line. Your organization simply cannot afford low engagement levels due to fuzzy standards or a cloudy company culture.

You need clarity. You need to clarify your culture, from recruitment to retirement and everything in between.

If this sounds like a lot of work remember that this is not an overnight process. Few worthwhile endeavors are ever quick or easy. Developing a culture of engagement through character requires lots of heart, and lots of intention and determination. It requires lots of thought.

Let's return to the **Character Model**.

Thoughts

Good character is more to be praised than outstanding talent. Most talents are, to some extent, a gift. Good character, by contrast, is not given to us. We have to build it piece by piece–by thought, choice, courage, and determination.

John Luther

How does the leadership team harvest and manage their thoughts, perspectives and insights regarding the engagement culture? In what format does communication flow in order to ensure ongoing improvements and problem solving?

How all the leaders share thoughts, ideas, and information among themselves and with their teams will be a function of how your leadership team plans to create a culture of engagement, and your organization's existing information channels and systems.

You also have to address the existing culture in your organization. Are your employees currently accustomed to sharing information? If so, in what manner is information shared–email, meetings, intranet? Do your teams value information?

Understanding how your employees think is crucial to putting in place a strategy of engagement through character. From character principles right through to effective behaviors, engagement is about how we treat people. This is fundamental, for whatever organizational approach your leadership uses to make sure information flows smoothly and effectively, there will be no avoiding the fact that you and the other leaders will be dealing with emotions. How people think is intertwined with how they feel, both on the individual level and on the collective level, presenting a challenge to even the best of leaders.

REALITY BITES

A Technical Man (or Woman) of the People?

Senior leaders often promote people to leadership positions on the basis of their technical skill sets, overlooking a lack of people skills. Yes, some industries are more technology heavy than others, but the fact remains that leaders lead people and manage processes: People show up to work, delight in making a contribution, eat lunch, and, in many cases, people get choked up when they retire.

People are often happiest when in a state called "flow," according to Professor Mihaly Csikszentmihalyi, author of *Living Well*. Flow is the state that occurs when your body and mind are totally absorbed in a task that is appropriately challenging. Therefore, many people are happier at work than at play. "After the flow experience is over, you look back on it, and in retrospect, it feels like it was real happiness," writes Csikszentmihalyi.[5]

Though it may not be your job to define and supply complete and utter happiness for your employees or for your organization, it is your responsibility as a leader to engage people–whole individuals with complex emotions–so that they are committed to their work and aligned with the character of your organization. That means understanding their emotions. It means, yes, empathy.

Feelings

Character cannot be developed in ease and quiet. Only through experience of trial and suffering can the soul be strengthened, vision cleared, ambition inspired, and success achieved.

Helen Keller

Emotions are part of us whether we want them or not, and they can be as powerful in a world where money and careers are involved as they are in our personal lives. Oftentimes, however, they hinder our intentions by leading us to behave in undesirable and unintended ways.

MAKING THE WORST OF IT

According to the Ivey Business Journal, strong negative emotions in the workplace have a serious impact on employee productivity and performance. Those who feel frustrated, guilty, angry, or humiliated, will often become defensive, seeking to withdraw from or compete with co-workers. Over time such toxic emotions lead people to destructive behaviors and office politics, which cause physical and mental stress, and even psychosomatic disorders. The outcome is an increase in health care costs and a decrease in our society's economic performance.[6]

An engaging culture means that there is a fundamental sense of safety, satisfaction, pride, ownership, excitement, enjoyment, and fulfillment among the majority of employees the majority of the time.

Naturally, there will be moments of irritation, upset, frustration, and so on. The key is that leaders recognize and respond sincerely and appropriately to these feelings (both in themselves and others) in order to ensure that morale and engagement levels remain high.

REALITY BITES

Office Bash: A Culture of Fear

ABC Company starts every week with a sales meeting, with sales people calling in from all over the world. They often dread the call-in, as they know their sales manager has already made aggressive revenue promises to "the street" and will now attempt to achieve his targets by berating, belittling and humiliating his team. The callers spend the hour holding their breath, waiting tensely for a question to come their way and being scrupulously careful with every word they utter.

After the "weekly flogging" is finished, the team members call each other to try and recover. By conversing with one another they manage to offer the mutual support necessary to help them refocus and get on with the task of selling. One of the sales people, my coaching client, has told me it takes about two days to get past the call and move on, so emotionally bruised is the team by the end of it. She and the majority of the team are looking for other work. No surprise.

This is a clear example of a manager who has adopted a disengaging style. Your success as a leader, and the success of your team, depends upon your emotional intelligence.

Your ability to be a healthy, effective peer as well as leader depends on your ability to understand and manage your emotions and respond effectively to emotions around you. This is your path to increasing engagement and creating teams that produce great results.

Research collected by the Consortium for Research on Emotional Intelligence in Organizations shows that salespeople, military recruiters, and executives who scored higher on written Emotional Intelligence tests outperformed and out-earned colleagues who scored lower.[7]

As a leader you have to ask yourself, when it is acceptable to be openly angry? Who is allowed to show their anger, fear, frustration, delight, etc; and how are individuals expected to behave when others are expressing strong emotions? How will you handle mistakes?

Members of the leadership team will have to ask themselves the same questions, to govern their relationships while creating and maintaining the organizational culture. This will require vision, as the leaders will have to come to a common understanding of how emotions work in a culture of engagement. Expect to be challenged.

The strong and focused communication skills required by the **Leadership Engagement Behaviors** can make your job an emotional roller coaster. While some people seem born with people prowess, few of us were born and/or raised in a place of work. How we treat others in the workplace so that they feel engaged and ready to perform requires practice and experience. It also requires clear purpose, training, and support.

It is your character that will see you through the ups and downs of the learning process of leadership, helping you behave as you intend.

Behaviors: Organizational Words and Actions

If you want others to be happy, practice compassion. If you want to be happy, practice compassion.

The Dalai Lama

Returning to the **Character Model**, we come to Behavior, where our intentions work for us or they don't. Though intentions make for a powerful start on the path to creating a culture of engagement, we need the right behaviors in order to finish successfully.

Organizational Engagement Actions

1. Put the systems in place to support leaders as they learn and practice the **Leadership Engagement Behaviors** (meetings to clarify intentions and deal with barriers. Provide mentors and coaches).
2. Start with the Senior Leadership Team. The leadership defines, in behavioral terms, what they do and say to practice courage, honesty, compassion, authenticity, inclusiveness and fairness while implementing the **Leadership Engagement Behaviors**. That means with each other as well as with the teams they lead.
3. Have a communication plan which identifies what the organization is trying to achieve and why.
4. Measure the current situation.
5. Train leaders in engagement skills.
6. Support leaders with feedback.
7. Measure engagement levels after a period of time (6 months).
8. Correlate engagement levels to performance indicators (e.g. revenue increase, cost reduction).
9. Incorporate **Leadership Engagement Behaviors** into the Leadership Evaluation System.
10. Celebrate achievements.

The ultimate outcome of clarifying the culture is a workplace that has set the stage for engagement. Mind you, "all," is a rather grand task for any one leader to address on any given day.

To help us see how clarifying the culture works on an individual level, let's take a look at a case study to see how a leader might proactively and intentionally use the **Character Model** to explicitly address behavioral issues and build character in the workplace.

Paula versus Sam

Paula, a new supervisor, loses her cool and shouts at Sam, who is having difficulty performing a task. Paula's leader overhears the incident and asks to talk to her about it.

Knowing that insight is the first step toward making change, the leader considers a range of questions to ask Paula. Here are just some of the possibilities:

Overall Character Perspective:

- Paula, what just happened with Sam?

Intentions:

- What do you believe is the right approach when someone is having trouble doing their work? How do you wish to be approached?
- What are your beliefs around the appropriateness of shouting at someone? When is this acceptable behavior? When is it not?
- How do you want your staff to see you as their leader?

Thoughts:

- Is this the way you intended to handle the situation?
- What went through your mind before you talked to Sam?
- Do you plan discussions ahead of time or work them out as you go along?
- How do you factor in the communication style of the other person before trying to engage him or her in a challenging discussion?
- How aware are you of your body language and that of others?

- How are people reacting to your approach?

Feelings:

- In what situations do you feel you lose control? And what are the physical clues that your emotions are getting the better of you?
- What did you notice about Sam's emotional state? How do you think he is feeling right now? And how may it impact his work?

Behaviors (Words and Actions):

- What process or model do you use for offering constructive feedback?
- What can you do now to sort things out with Sam?

By using the **Character Model**, Paula and her leader start asking the right questions and really start to pinpoint where difficulties and disharmony may exist, and why. In doing so they are showing how leaders can understand and influence their organizational culture. Paula, having been given specific and explicit feedback from her own leader, now has an opportunity to think about the changes she can make to build her character, engage her team, and strengthen her leadership.

Over time, as leaders address situations using the **Character Model**, a culture of engagement will evolve, in which each and every employee in the organization behaves in an aligned manner.

So, what does it look like when an organization has completely and successfully clarified their culture? What is the legacy?

REALITY BITES

Bill's Legacy: Character, Compassion, and Complete Success.

A few years ago, I was working with an organization when their leader, Bill, was retiring. The man was tremendously well liked, which was abundantly evident in the number of readily offered "Bill stories" during his retirement dinner. One speaker's story was emblematic of Bill's character: "One night after work my car wouldn't start. Bill was the only person left in the building. I told him what happened. He threw me the keys to his car, told me to keep it for the night. He lived near by and could walk home. There is nothing I wouldn't do for this man and this company." Others recounted how Bill took such a sincere interest in the lives of his employees and their families that he could remember names, dates, and events. No one talked about the fact that this was a tremendously successful company (though it was). They just talked about Bill's kindness and sincerity.

This is the legacy of character.

Bill's company exemplifies how clarifying the culture can result in an organization in which compassion, trust, and character reign, and where engagement is the norm.

Clearly, from intentions right through to engagement behaviors, there are opportunities to clarify your organizational culture, to build a culture of engagement through character using the **Character Model**. By doing nothing, something will still happen–it just might not be the outcome you were hoping for. Don't let that happen. There's too much on the line.

So, think about what you want to accomplish, envision a workplace in which engagement and trust are the norm, and get to work.

Recap of Thoughts

Clarifying the culture is about you and the other leaders in your organization addressing organizational principles, values, goals, and objectives. It's about asking what sort of thoughts and feelings and behaviors describe the culture your leadership team intends to create. It's about intentionally creating a culture in which character-based engagement behaviors are practiced consistently, everyday.

Putting It into Words and Actions

The scope of this chapter is undoubtedly broad as well as deep. You may be wondering where you should start. Below are three steps you can take to begin determining to what extent engagement fits into your organization's current culture, and how you can begin creating a culture of engagement through character.

In the same way we ended the last chapter by asking you to assess your organization, we again ask you to take an honest look at your team.

1. Clarifying Your Current Culture

How do you (and others) describe the current culture?

What is your assessment of the current state of engagement?

Fully Engaged _____%

Moderately Engaged_____%

Disengaged_____%

2. Leadership by Engagement Organizational Character Audit

Revisit the subject of your organizational **Beliefs**. Take action on them by asking yourself about your team's **Principles**:

- Do we believe that it is important to engage people?
  Are the **Leadership Engagement Behaviors** applicable for our environment?
- If not, what makes sense?
- Do we, the leadership team members treat each other in an engaging manner?
- Is it important that we are all aligned before we start working with our direct reports on engagement issues?
- Do we believe that we must understand and align our own character to apply the **Leadership Engagement Behaviors**?
- How do we ensure that each person understands his or her role in achieving departmental/organizational alignment?
- What do we believe about training leaders to create a more engaging culture?
- How do we hold leaders accountable to practice the **Leadership Engagement Behaviors**?
- Do we include the **Leadership Engagement Behaviors** as part of the leadership evaluation process?
- What do we do when leaders do not meet our standards?
- How do we measure engagement?
- What indicators do we correlate to in order to evaluate concrete results?

Beliefs are a great start, but in order to energize your team, you also need to have concrete **Goals** in place.

Ask yourself about your organizational **Priorities:**

- What are your leadership priorities in creating a culture of engagement?
- How do you balance the need to produce tangible outcomes while maintaining an engaging culture?
- Who should be aware of this process?

Ask yourself about your organizational **Objectives**:

- How do the priorities transform into organizational objectives?
- What is the strategy?
- What is the plan?
- How will you communicate the plan? To leaders? To all team members?
- Who is responsible for what?
- How do we inspire all the team leaders to embrace the self-discipline required in applying the **Character Model** and in practicing the **Leadership Engagement Behaviors**?
- How will you measure our success?
- How can you establish milestones?
- How will you celebrate?

3. Organizational Engagement Actions

Finally, act on what the foregoing questions have taught you about your organization:

- Put the systems in place to support leaders as they learn and practice the **Leadership Engagement Behaviors** (meetings to clarify intentions and deal with barriers, mentors, coaches).
- Start with the Senior Leadership Team. The leadership defines, in behavioral terms, what they do and say to practice courage, honesty, compassion, authenticity, inclusiveness and fairness while implementing the **Leadership Engagement Behaviors**. That means with each other as well as with the teams they lead.
- Have a communication plan that identifies what the organization is trying to achieve and why.

- Measure the current situation.
- Train leaders in engagement skills.
- Support leaders with feedback.
- Measure engagement levels after a period of time (6 months).
- Correlate engagement levels to performance indicators (revenue increase, cost reduction).
- Incorporate the **Leadership Engagement Behaviors** into the Leadership Evaluation System.
- Celebrate achievements.

We also looked at the need to put in place effective hiring and communication strategies so that all of your employees clearly understand where your organization wants to go, how it wants to get there, and what role each of them plays creating a culture of engagement–of extraordinary results.

This last point is not frivolous stuff. As you will learn in this book and in practice, celebrating what you have achieved is a powerful way to strengthen the culture of engagement you have built while ensuring you continue to attract, retain, and energize your team.

In the next chapter, Know Your Character, we will look at what you need to consider about yourself as an individual in order to proactively align yourself with your organization, move forward and become an authentically engaging leader!

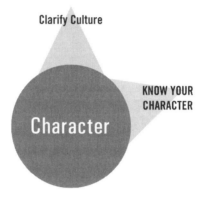

Clarify Culture

KNOW YOUR
CHARACTER

Character

The intention of Know Your Character is to provide an in-depth exploration of the **Character Model**. This model will assist you in two ways: It will allow you to consider whether you are a match for your organization, and it will help you manage your character in order to engage your team.

Knowing your character means you will be in a better position to attract, retain, and energize your team, because you will know what makes you tick as a person and what engages you as a leader.

Intentional Acts of Character
Paternity Pull

George, a senior leader, was adopted when he was a baby. Growing up, he was keenly aware of his value within his family and therefore developed a heartfelt appreciation for the importance of children and parenting. So when he and his wife had their second baby, he decided to take the extended paternity leave available to fathers. Though his choice was no surprise to those who knew George well, many at work raised eyebrows at the decision, as George was the first man there to make such a move.

When his paternity leave was over, George made another important decision. His job required him to travel extensively, for days or sometimes weeks at a time–far too much time for a man like George to spend away from his children on a regular basis. So, he requested and received a demotion in order to work closer to home. When his children began going to school, George approached his leader at the time and told her his lifestyle had changed and he could devote more time to work. The organization showed its character: George was promoted to his old job and everyone benefited from having their former leader back, now more engaged than ever.

Know Your Character

Do not wish to be anything but what you are, and try to be that perfectly.

St. Francis De Sales

Earlier we asked: How can you lead others if you cannot lead yourself? In order to create an engaging culture at work, you have to look at who you are as a leader.

There are two critical issues at hand: first, your compatibility with your workplace culture; second, leveraging your character to enhance engagement.

Are you a match with your organization? Does your current organizational culture support engagement?

At some point in our lives many of us took a job simply because we needed one. We molded ourselves as best as possible to the requirements of the position and culture of the organization. That was then.

Due to the changing workplace and the lack of stigma in changing jobs and professions, many of us have more choice regarding how we earn a living. We can choose to work in environments that support our values and talents. This gives us more of an opportunity to work proactively, intentionally, according to our character–to work at our best.

To do your best work, your character must be aligned with the character of your organization, starting at the inner core–intentions–yours and theirs.

Ask yourself the following three questions:

1. Does my organization believe that it is important to engage employees?
2. Do we, as a leadership team, understand the connection between levels of engagement and organizational results?
3. Is the leadership prepared to do the work required to increase the engagement level in our workplace?

If you can answer *yes* to these questions your organization is on the path to increasing engagement. You, as a leader, can then apply the concepts in the **Character Model** to ensure your alignment.

If some or all of the answers are *no* you have more questions to address to understand your organization's appetite for engagement:

1. Clarify the intentions of the organization.
2. Can you lead your team according to what you believe to be true, honorable and fair?
3. If you truly believe that you are mismatched with the organization, talk to your own leader, human resources, or individuals whom you trust. Is there an opportunity to rethink intentions at an organizational level? What is the future for this organization if you/they ignore the issue of engagement?

The worst case scenario is that you will have to make a choice. If you are mismatched with the organizational culture you will continue to suffer inner conflict, feel disconnected and disengaged. If, on the other hand, there is genuine desire for engagement, get ready to engage!

Leveraging Your Character for Engagement

Character is like a tree and reputation like a shadow. The shadow is what we think of it; the tree is the real thing.

Abraham Lincoln

Once you know that your organization is truly striving to engage its employees, the next step is to leverage your character to maximize your ability to engage your team. You wouldn't build a home with wonky tools. Nor should you try to create a culture of engagement without clear and solid intentions. The **Character Model** is a powerful tool that will help you lead effectively, engagingly, authentically–from the inside out.

Your Character

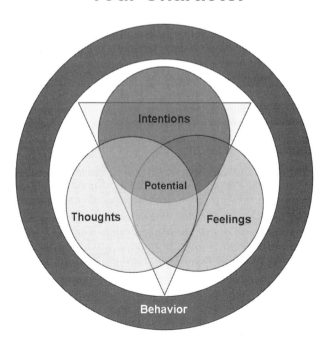

Intentions: Every Day and in Every Way

That which dominates our imaginations and our thoughts will determine our lives, and our character.

Ralph Waldo Emerson

We often ask participants in our management training sessions, "What do you want to achieve?" Surprisingly, they often answer, "I don't know, I was sent here" or "whatever you have to teach me." Why would a true leader give all that power away?

Suppose you are asked to attend a training session. You have an opportunity to decide what is important to you. The more you think about your own goals and priorities, the better. You are taking control of your working life. When you assert your request and make your intentions known, you will be perceived as a leader with purpose. Would you board a ship where the captain says, "Ah, wherever the wind takes us?"

Similar to training sessions, your employees should know what the organization, your department and what they are trying to achieve themselves. Otherwise, they won't know how they fit, which will create a culture of confusion, annoyance, and disengagement. Neither you nor they will know how to navigate the rough waters when challenging situations arise. Is this the sort of workplace you want?

Intention in Challenging Interactions

You are quite likely aware of sensitive and potentially volatile interactions in your workplace. When offering constructive feedback, problem solving on a recurring problem, or "speaking up to power," it is extremely important that you think through what you are trying to achieve, even before scheduling a discussion. This may sound simple but it isn't. People often dive into difficult conversations with little thought or awareness of their objectives for the interaction.

To behave the way you intend you must be aligned from the inside out. This requires not only awareness and skill but also disciplined thinking.

Thoughts

Cognitive intelligence describes your ability to solve problems, gather facts, and to reason. Your thinking process supports every layer of who you are, as the elements of your character are interdependent and intertwined. They work as a whole, providing clues and cues to help you understand yourself as person and as a leader. Pay attention to your thoughts and feelings, reevaluate your beliefs, and honor your many strengths, talents, and preferences. You will improve your ability to lead according to your intentions. However, cognition is not a quick and easy process, as it demands honesty, time, and discipline.

But the brain will help, according to Dr. Norman Doidge, author of *The Brain that Changes Itself.* Doidge asserts that the brain's anatomy is not fixed. Rather, it is flexible or "plastic," allowing us to learn, raise our IQ, and reverse deterioration. We can even train our brains to be happier.[1]

Learning how to align your behavior to support your intentions is a continuous process, but it means you have to slow the world down just a little bit.

REALITY BITES

A Reflection of You as a Leader

Some people are reluctant to consider the **Character Model**, rigid in their assertion that they are who they are and that second guessing themselves is just a waste of time. Not so. People who avoid reflection run the risk of remaining in reactive mode. Without reflection, people tend to believe that other people and events are responsible for the way they act. Again, why on earth would you give away all that power?

Think about It

The unexamined life is not worth living.

Socrates

Reflection is not navel gazing but the foundation of self-care and self-management. The healthy, dynamic leader continually refines his or her skills through self-mastery, which requires self-knowledge.

Enter your mind's secret powerhouse–intuition. This continuous interplay between your senses and your memory (conscious and unconscious) creates a release of chemicals that provides you with vital information for making decisions on a gut level.

Like any powerful force, the body's reactions must be understood if they are to be managed. Reflection and reason help you to factor your feelings into your decision making so that you will be confident your choices are aligned with your intentions, with what you want to achieve in the long run and at a particular moment in time. But how do you interpret all this physiological information in the first place and at any given time?

Feelings–In the Heat of the Moment

Feelings can be positive, negative, and neutral. What we are talking about here are feelings that provoke a significant self-protective reaction.

What are your flash points and triggers? Which people and/or circumstances get a rise out of you? When do you feel that *you lose it*?

One night a loud sound frightens you. Blood rushes from your brain, your heart begins racing, adrenalin pumps into your blood, and your muscles tighten for action as your survival mechanism prepares you for your two immediate choices: fight or flight.

While this primal adaptation may be necessary for the continuation of our species, it can set in motion some awfully nasty and disengaging behaviors.

A leader who flees or roars guttural battle cries when stressed out may not achieve what he or she intends!

While, thankfully, most work encounters are much less dramatic than the above scenario, there are moments when we feel as though we are being emotionally hijacked.

How can you master the fight-or-flight reaction, to keep powerful emotions from thwarting your otherwise well-intentioned plans?

Fortunately, as relatively evolved, thinking beings, we do have a third option to fight or flight, and it is called **SNIP**. Remember that triangle in the **Character Model**, the one mentioned in the first chapter? This is it.

SNIP before You Go

SNIP (Stop, Notice, Inquire, and Plan) is a proven self-management tool that can help you interrupt immediate and potentially destructive reactions and replace them with intentional, conscious, and productive choices. **SNIP** can help you align your intentions, thoughts, feelings, and actions, to achieve desired results.

SNIP Triangle

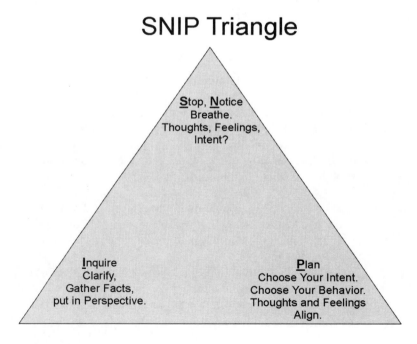

Stop, Notice
Breathe.
Thoughts, Feelings,
Intent?

Inquire
Clarify,
Gather Facts,
put in Perspective.

Plan
Choose Your Intent.
Choose Your Behavior.
Thoughts and Feelings
Align.

SNIP helps you align the elements of your character–intentions, thoughts, feelings, and behavior–so that they work together, equipping us with effective tools for self-mastery *before, during, and after* stressful situations. It has value both proactively and reactively.

Reactively speaking, when you find yourself in a stressful situation and at risk of behaving in an unintended manner, using **SNIP** can help you apply the **Character Model** by giving you time to consider your intention in a given situation, your thoughts and your feelings, so that you can then choose the most appropriate and engaging behavior.

Proactively speaking, **SNIP** is a powerful tool when you are getting ready to meet with someone. The same approach applies–Stop, Notice, Inquire, and Plan–but in this case you would be using **SNIP** as a strategic, long-term tool for engagement.

Here's how **SNIP** works:

Leveraging Character with a SNIP

Here are some tips to help you get the jump on your emotions, align your behavior with your intentions, and turn what might have been a disaster into an engaging encounter:

Before SNIP

- *Expect emotions.* They are part of being human. But hiding your emotions confuses people, so allow yourself to express them in an appropriate way.
- *Anticipate.* What can happen that might evoke an emotional reaction?
- *Visualize.* Imagine success. What does it look like? See it, smell it, taste it and feel it.
- *Prepare.* You are more vulnerable when you are tired, hungry, or stressed out, so make sure you are well rested and calm. Do your homework (when possible) to have the information you need, words you might want to say etc.
- *Practice.* Practice responses to behaviors that may cause you to react emotionally.
- *Trust.* Clarify your intention, what you are trying to achieve, and know that people often interpret your thoughts and actions differently than you intend. Trust that your intentions are right.

During SNIP

- *Apply SNIP.* Stop, Notice, Inquire and Plan.
- **Stop.** If you feel yourself spiraling out of control, stop and reschedule the conversation. You can say "give me a minute to think here" or "can we slow this down a bit. I need to think about this before continuing."
- **Notice.** Pay attention to your physical reactions. You are likely breathing shallowly. So take deeper breaths, look away for a moment, and then begin when you are ready. What would you name the sensation?
- **Inquire.** Ask questions of the other person to gain time and control. "Tell me more." "Can you give me an example?" "What has this been like for you?"
- *Empathize.* Mirror the other person's emotion and content to ensure understanding. "Sounds like you are angry that this happened again." "I see you are upset that the numbers are inaccurate."
- *Change your physical position.* If you are standing, shift your weight; if you are sitting, readjust yourself–this allows the blood to flow in a different way. Be mindful not to take an aggressive posture. If possible, inject humor into the conversation. Laughter lightens!
- *Think gratitude.* Think about something for which you are very grateful. It will change your mindset and therefore your reactions.
- **Plan.** Now that you have clarified your intention in this moment and calmed yourself, what is the best thing to say or do to yield your desired outcome? Proceed with your clarified insight.

But, thoughts and emotions during encounters happen in the blink of an eye, you may argue. True. But that doesn't mean you have to be ruled by them. **SNIP** is about mastering and marshaling your character, by giving your behavior time to catch up to and align with your intentions. Stay in character–your character.

This leads us to an important consideration: Are you a person who is driven by thoughts? Many of us were raised or trained with the notion that thoughts are more significant than feelings, and yet others of us are moved more by emotions than logic. Which describes you?

Knowing your character means knowing what makes you tick, and while the point here is not to place value judgments on one type of response or the other, being too much of either can lead you out of alignment and away from engagement.

We've already introduced you to a **Character Model** in which intentions, thoughts, and feelings are balanced and aligned to produce engaging behaviors; this is a model with healthy Character Potential.

Here's another look:

Your Character

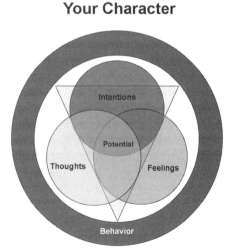

What happens when thoughts and feelings aren't aligned? What does misalignment within the **Character Model** look like?

Let's take a look.

When You Are a Little Heavy on the Thoughts

Your Character

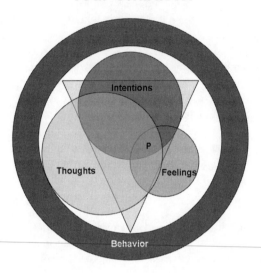

When feelings are ignored or dismissed as unimportant (yours or the person you are interacting with), you will not only miss chances to understand your actions and reactions, and therefore your emotional self, but you will shrink your Character Potential and the opportunity to engage your team.

The result will be good intentions and problem solving without emotional awareness, which is half of the solution.

Now let's look at the other end of the spectrum within the **Character Model**.

When You Need to Lighten Up on the Feelings

Your Character

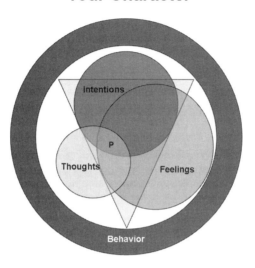

When your feelings dominate your character, or the situation at hand, you can lose sight of the problem you are trying to solve.

And as we said earlier, losing sight can happen instantaneously, without too much warning–so quickly that you may wonder how you can possibly distinguish between the thoughts and feelings you are experiencing, and how you can master them.

REALITY BITES

Which Came First–the Thought or the Feeling?

It depends. Sometimes a thought will pop into my mind and I realize how I really feel. Or, conversely, I feel that internal flip and grasp that there is something going on I must pay attention to. Thoughts and feelings happen so quickly that mastering my behavior can be a real challenge. The key is to stop, not react by doing or saying something I might regret. Next, I breathe (deeply), ask questions or clarify what was said, and consider the best possible outcome of the situation, and then proceed with caution.

It sounds trite but it rhymes and is easy to remember: **"When I feel the flip, it's time to SNIP."**

Remembering Paula and Sam from chapter two, we can now see that Paula could have applied **SNIP** when she felt "the flip" while dealing with Sam. With **SNIP,** Paula would also be able to plan for future dealings with him, aligning her intentions, thoughts, feelings, and behavior, so that her character is integrated and working to produce intended results.

After SNIP

- *Exercise*. Help your body process the chemical reaction.
- *Drink (water)*. Drink water to flush out your system
- *Rest*. Being emotionally upset puts a strain on the body's systems, take time to rest and refresh yourself before moving on to other things in your day.
- *Consider another's criticism.* There may be some part of what you heard that you could benefit from.
- *Reflect*. Think about what happened, what you did correctly and what you will do differently in the future. Overreacting to an everyday event is an indication that you are really reacting to something in your history. Take time to process old emotions when they emerge.
- *Get support*. Talk with a trusted, caring, supportive person to ensure you maintain a good perspective and to help you brainstorm constructive and aligned solutions.
- *Do something you enjoy*. Perhaps you like nature trails, gardening, writing or reading, or sports.

This last point is serious, not fluff. Self-expression is a fundamental part of human nature, and when it is denied we feel stressed. Doing what we enjoy gives us perspective on life, develops our talents, and makes us grounded and more effective at work.

And if you enjoy what you do at work, and who you are at work, you will be more than effective: you will be engaging.

Your Personality at Work

How often have you felt that you are not your complete or true self at work? This is not an uncommon realization. Many people learn to be "someone else" on the job. The question is who are they? Someone they think they have to be? You simply cannot engage others when you are hiding.

You are unique, and something about who you are got you to where you are right now. Healthy character is not a "one size fits all" way of being. Neither is **Leadership by Engagement**. It is your configuration and yours alone.

You have talents, gifts, and approaches that are yours. If you don't know what they are, ask some people who care about you (though perhaps not your mother). What unique strengths do you possess as a person and as a leader? How can you leverage these strengths to even greater advantage?

The old philosophy was that we tried to "develop" people to become perfect corporate entities. Uniformity may be desirable for the surface of a boardroom table, or that of a pool table, but in a corporate team, sameness is not perfection. Fortunately, we now understand that successful organizations are built by uniquely talented people doing what they do best.

REALITY BITES

Jobs on Jobs

Steve Jobs, CEO of Apple Computer and of Pixar Animation Studios, knows about living and succeeding from the inside out. When he addressed a graduating class at Stanford University in June 2005, Jobs, a college dropout, stressed the vital role intuition plays in guiding his decisions, even if it means abandoning some endeavors, and how loving his work and being himself has seen him through the biggest of life's challenges.

"I'm convinced that the only thing that kept me going was that I loved what I did," said Jobs. "You've got to find what you love. And that is as true for your work as it is for your lovers. Your work is going to fill a large part of your life, and the only way to be truly satisfied is to do what you believe is great work."[2]

Though few of us will rise to international prominence by following our hearts, there is no disputing that our feelings can provide us with vital information and help us decide if we are where we should be. Not only will this create a sense of harmony between you and your work environment, but it will also impact your performance.

Your Behavior–Communicating for Best Results

This outer layer of your character is the manifestation of all your inner elements, your personality included. Your behavior is what you say and do, and how you say it and do it.

Let's return to an essential question we asked in the first chapter: What qualities make someone an excellent leader? Engaging leadership is about how leaders treat people, and it always boils down to the **Leadership Engagement Behaviors**.

To reiterate, the list is not a prescription for conformity or uniformity. The **Leadership Engagement Behaviors** describe the key fundamental behaviors that will help you engage your team, in concert with your unique talents and style. In fact, your organization needs your unique gifts.

However, it takes discipline to be yourself, tap into your gifts, and behave according to your true character.

REALITY BITES

Discipline: The Glue of Character

For the past six years I have worked hard to apply the **Character Model** in my daily life. My objective is to be sure that it works and that I understand all the nuances. Having applied it to everything from communication in difficult moments to managing my weight, I have discovered that the glue holding together this interactive, interwoven character approach to self-management is discipline.

Discipline requires for me to notice my thoughts and link them back to my intention in every situation; to pay attention to the physical reactions alerting me to potential detours from my goals; to manage my words and my body language in significant interactions.

My goal is to manage my character in a way that truly represents who I want to be. And that requires ongoing vigilance.

One of the biggest gifts of self-management through character is the feeling of delight and empowerment when I keep promises I've made to myself. The payoff is that my self-esteem and confidence have grown. Without discipline the **Character Model** is just a philosophical notion. Discipline is the glue that holds it together and keeps it working.

Leading by engagement requires that you understand who you are, exercise self-discipline, and leverage *your authentic character.*

Recap of Thoughts

Knowing your character is about leading yourself so that you can lead others, and it requires that you address a key consideration: Are you matched with your organization? After honestly answering this simple question you find yourself faced with two vastly different outcomes: Either you will end up leaving your company, which in light of what we've read may not be the worst case scenario after all, or you will decide to stay and help others create a culture of engagement.

We also looked at the self-discipline, skill, and determination that character engagement requires, and how reflection and self-knowledge can help you master your intentions, thoughts, feelings, and behavior with the help of the **Character Model** and **SNIP**.

Finally, we looked at what inspires people to perform at their best. By following your intuition and your true nature, you will align yourself with your organization, lead with greater satisfaction and happiness, and achieve extraordinary results.

Putting It into Words and Actions

Knowing your character is not necessarily about sitting on a rock in the desert, though it may be less painful than that, as most workplaces have proper chairs. And, we can offer you some direction.

Below are the key highlights of what we have discussed in this chapter, measures you can take to actively get to know who you are in stressful or challenging situations.

1. Character for Engagement

What have you learned about your "Intention" in significant conversations and situations?

How are you managing the interplay between your thoughts and feelings?

How is this rigorous effort impacting your words and actions, particularly in relation to the **Leadership Engagement Behaviors**?

2. Applying SNIP

As we have seen, **SNIP** is a process for moving away from having a reaction to someone/something to a considered, proactive leadership approach.

When you feel the flip, it's time to SNIP.

What are your indicators that something is amiss? When you feel the flip, you need to stop and think about what is happening rather than just proceeding in the moment. You might say you have to audit the situation.

Flip Audit

Is your heart racing?

Is your breathing shallow?

Is your gut in opposition to your head?

Are you racing to rationalize what you (or someone else) are doing?

Are you at a loss for words?

Do you feel like screaming?

Are you having an emotional reaction?

Do you just feel that something is wrong?

Do you want to flee the scene?

Don't flee! Use the power of language. We know the look and feel of **SNIP**, but what does it sound like?

Putting SNIP into Words

"I need to stop and think for a moment. I would like to continue this conversation at a later time."

"I'm uncomfortable with what is happening. I want to take a bit of time to think this through."

"Let's stop for moment and get some air. I want to focus my thoughts."

"I want to think about this to be sure that I'm making the best choice/decision."

"This is not appropriate. I'm ending this conversation."

The next time that you are anticipating a challenging, emotionally charged situation employ the **"Before, During and After"** SNIP practices we looked at earlier in the chapter.

Determine if these practices help you align your actions and words with your character/engagement intentions. Engaging others requires self-control, which in turn requires self-awareness and self-discipline.

By applying **SNIP** when necessary you will develop the self-mastery required to retain and energize your team members.

In our next chapter, Respect Yourself, we will look at your own level of engagement and how establishing boundaries, resisting manipulation, and self-respect are essential to self-care and authentic leadership and engagement.

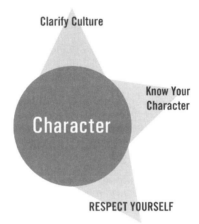

Clarify Culture

Know Your
Character

Character

RESPECT YOURSELF

The intention of Respect Yourself is to help you determine and maintain your own level of engagement, and to give you the tools you need for keeping your balance in the give and take of your leadership position.

Respect Others shows us that engagement is a two-way street. If you are going to attract, retain, and energize your team members, you must stay engaged yourself.

Intentional Acts of Character
Candid Conversations

Laura Falby, Director of People Development for Second Cup, described her surprise at the honest comments coming from her direct reports: "My younger team members tell me openly and candidly that they are not particularly concerned about promotion and pay. Also, they are clear with me that they will leave if they are not challenged and learning. I can't imagine hearing these messages ten years ago. Some may've felt this way, but no one would have been so forthright. Even though hearing this information catches me off guard, I appreciate it. Now I know that it's incumbent on me to involve my team members whenever possible, and present them with opportunities that will enrich their experience here and increase their engagement–for their good and the good of the organization."

Respect Yourself

To be what we are, and to become what we are capable of becoming, is the only end of life.

Robert Louis Stevenson

How Engaged Are You?

In The Core, we established why engagement is necessary. In Clarify the Culture, we looked at how you can create a foundation for higher engagement where you work. Then, in Know Your Character, we asked you if engagement is possible in your organization, and how the Character Model can be used to bring out your best.

Now we ask: How can you assess, maintain, and enhance your level of engagement?

In a word, respect. It's fundamental to healthy character, the **Leadership Engagement Behaviors,** and all successful human endeavors. Quite simply, respect makes it possible for people to work well together. And while showing respect sounds simple in theory, in practice it requires discipline and care on your part – not only for others but for yourself as well. You need to stay engaged to engage others.

Self-respect protects your well-being by making sure you are engaged, from the inside out. If you don't feel engaged at your organization your passion will wane, as will your ability to lead your team effectively. A lack of self-respect has a ripple effect in your workplace.

BlessingWhite's research into engagement has found that managers who themselves are engaged are better able to engage their team members.[1]

Not sure if you are truly engaged? Clarify your level of engagement with a short quiz. Complete our Engagement Quiz to determine *your* level of engagement!

Go to: www.centreforcharacterleadership.com/engagequiz.htm.

How did you score?

If you are passionately engaged, celebrate. But if you are moderately engaged, determine what you can do to pump up your engagement level. Finally, if you are in the disengaged range, ask yourself if you are with the right organization for you. If you decide to stick it out where you are, talk to your leader about options. And if you decide to leave, search for an organization that is committed to engaging their people, where your character and self-respect are valued. These qualities are too important to squander on the wrong workplace.

Being and remaining engaged is about self-respect, self-care, and self-assurance. It is about establishing and maintaining your boundaries, resisting manipulation, and effectively dealing with the feedback you receive.

Practicing self-care (a concept that many people struggle with) is the ability to do what is right for you, to clarify your intentions, your purpose, principles, values, goals and objectives. Clarity will help you know when to say yes and when to say no, and how to keep yourself safe. Noticing your thoughts and feelings (and practicing **SNIP**) will help you to honor and respect yourself in your words and actions.

Everything can be taken from a man but . . . the last of human freedoms– to choose one's attitude to any given set of circumstances, to choose one's own way.

Victor Frankl

Don't Play Monkey in the Middle: Setting and Maintaining Boundaries

If you were ever the "monkey in the middle," you'll recall how pointless, humiliating, and frustrating it was to jump in vain for an object whose value was questionable to begin with. As a leader, if you're not careful, you can find yourself in the workplace equivalent of this game.

Leading to engagement, to achieve specific outcomes, requires understanding the complex dynamics of your team, the demands of your leaders, and the needs of your customers and shareholders. It requires balance–your balance.

Keeping your balance means respecting yourself enough not to get thrown by the demands of your role. It means setting and maintaining boundaries by distinguishing between your responsibilities and those of others. If you micromanage or protect people, you curtail their growth and run the risk that some employees will take advantage of you. If you neglect your leadership responsibilities, you leave people to sink or swim, which is evidence that you are not engaged. Self-respecting leaders also demonstrate respect for their team. It's a 50/50 deal.

REALITY BITES

You Are Responsible for 50 Percent of the Enchilada

For any One-on-One relationship to work, both individuals must be committed to success. While you can't make a relationship work on your own, you can do 100 percent of your part. As long as you faithfully keep your end of the bargain by practicing the **Leadership Engagement Behaviors**, by telling the other person the truth, and by offering them every chance to

contribute to the relationship and accept their choices, you will remain steady.

The **Leadership Engagement Behaviors** not only define the best leadership behaviors in the outer circle of the **Character Model**, but they describe your responsibilities as a leader.

You have responsibilities and your direct reports have responsibilities. It is about balance.

	Your responsibilities as leader	The responsibilities of your direct reports
1.	Treat people in a consistently civil manner.	Treat you in a consistently civil manner.
2.	Tell the truth.	Tell the truth to you.
3.	Listen openly with empathy.	Be open regarding issues impacting performance.
4.	Conduct yourself in an ethical manner.	Signal issues that create an ethical quandary.
5.	Create an atmosphere of camaraderie.	Participate as a team member.
6.	Provide autonomy to make decisions.	Make decisions.
7.	Articulate clear, measurable, achievable performance expectations.	Take responsibility to meet performance expectations and ask for help if required.
8.	Recognize contributions frequently, specifically and personally.	Explain how to best offer them recognition (privately, publicly, etc.).
9.	Address performance gaps in a timely, private, problem-solving manner.	Participate in problem solving discussions and bridge performance gaps.
10.	Provide opportunities for people to find challenge and significance in their work.	Determine and communicate what is challenging and significant.
11.	Ensure training and learning opportunities are available.	Apply new learning on the job.
12.	Provide proper tools and resources.	Utilize tools and resources where possible.

The way to maintain your balance and stay engaged is to remember that you can only do your best to meet your responsibilities. Going too far out on the **"Bridge of Understanding"** can leave you vulnerable to the rocks below. In your concern for your employees (and everyone else), you should never lose your concern for yourself.

REALITY BITES

The Overly Concerned Leader (taking the other half of the Enchilada)

Raj is a well-respected, long-time leader in a manufacturing plant. Firm, fair, and forthright, Raj often offers constructive criticism and praise in order to help his employees better themselves. Not everyone likes and respects him, however.

Some time ago, Raj learned that Tina, a woman on his team, had complained to his boss that he was being overly critical of her. Very concerned by this news, he decided to work on his communication. What troubled him was that his intentions and approach had always been good (or so he thought); he'd never had such a strong negative reaction from a direct report before, and wondered if the problem lay with Tina and how she receives feedback.

Raj can only keep his end of the bargain; be well-intentioned and as supportive, collaborative, and constructive in his communication as possible. He can't control how his message is received. The person on the receiving end, like the sender, has their own character. It may be that Tina will only see him negatively, and that is her choice. Being an effective communicator doesn't mean that everyone admires your skill. It means that you are clear in your positive intentions, manage your thoughts and feelings, and stay open to developing your skills. Raj is doing these things. What more can be asked of him?

Being a leader of authentic character means standing firm when you have done all you can to meet the other person without losing your balance and being afraid. Engagement, yours and theirs, will not happen from a position of fear and by taking overly cautious steps.

The beauty of balance is that you will know where you should be and when you are out of alignment with yourself. As a leader, you are likely familiar with the many situations in which your intentions are tested, when work dynamics threaten to lead you out of the circle of your character and into, well, a triangle.

Unlike **SNIP**, however, the following triangle is a bad one.

The Karpman Drama Triangle: Identifying and Resisting Manipulation

The **Karpman Drama Triangle** depicts interactions that are often played out among three notoriously negative players in the workplace–the Victim, the Persecutor, and the Rescuer.

This handy and helpful model shows how leaders can find themselves where they don't want to be. Behaving as a Rescuer, Victim and/or Persecutor invokes many, if not all aspects of the **Character Model**, because any place on the **Karpman Drama Triangle** is the wrong place to be! If you occupy any position on the triangle you are breaching boundaries and losing your balance, or taking it from others, and behaving in a disengaging manner– toward yourself and others.

THE KARPMAN DRAMA TRIANGLE

Leader as Rescuer:

"I can do it better myself."

"Leaders are paid more so we should not ask our people to do their work."

"I don't want my people to feel the same pressure that I am feeling."

"Leaders are supposed to have the answers."

Leader as Victim:

"Teammates just don't have the same level of responsibility as supervisors."

"I work more hours than anyone else."

"No one understands the pressure I am under."

"The union won't allow me to manage poor performance."

"It takes too long to deal with poor performance. I'd rather just turn a blind eye."

Leader as Persecutor:

"Young people don't have the same work ethic we did."

"I have to be tough to get the work done."

"It's my way or the highway."

"Do it now."

"I pay you to do, not think."

"Positive feedback! You get paid to do this work."

Staying off the Triangle

You keep off the triangle by working within the **Character Model** and by focusing on the **Leadership Engagement Behaviors.** This means respecting your own boundaries, treating others as functioning adults, and knowing your responsibilities and those of others. It means keeping your balance, and keeping your character intact.

Having established your balance through self-respect, you will be in the best position to lead with confidence. You will need it, for if you lead long enough, you will get input, positive and negative, from those around you. Be ready. Be steady. It's coming.

Receiving Feedback

Renowned basketball coach John Wooden believed it was a mistake to let yourself get "caught up" in praise or criticism. Similarly, as a leader, you must maintain your balance when receiving feedback.

Feedback from your Leader

Just as you're significantly implicated in the engagement of your team, so is your immediate leader implicated in your level of engagement. The way that your leader offers feedback is extremely important, and the **Character Model** offers a solid structure to help you evaluate the feedback you receive.

Feedback reveals a person's true intentions. Healthy intentions will be evident when feedback is given in a fair and supportive manner. A leader of good character can identify and learn to master her frustration, disappointment, and fear in order to offer feedback constructively. She can also factor in your personality, choose the best time to offer feedback, and use the most appropriate wording to achieve the best results from the conversation.

Unfortunately, not all encounters with leaders are well considered and positive.

REALITY BITES

Someone Woke up on the Wrong Side of the Office

One senior leader calls his boss a "dicta-terrorist" who wields his dictaphone in the early morning to write blistering memos to his staff. "You'd come in, sort of feeling good about yourself and feeling organized, and one of those frigging bombs would land on your desk. Well, they just came short of saying bad things about your mother. They were soul destroying and the whole world would get copied" says the chastened leader.

Remember, it is never acceptable to allow yourself to be humiliated, abused, degraded, or shamed. If you do feel this way, exercise your self-respect, assert your boundaries, and stop the conversation.

While receiving feedback from your immediate leader may be a daunting test of your balance, you will also be tested by other people in the organization. So, look around you, and be prepared!

Receiving Feedback from Other Directions

We do not see the world as it is. We see the world as we are.

The Talmud

As a leader, you may think of yourself as an unmitigated success. Or, perhaps you see yourself as an abject failure. The truth undoubtedly lies somewhere between these two extremes. The good news is that you can learn the truth (at least the perceptions, if not the intention) about how well you are doing as a leader.

Twenty-five years ago leaders offered feedback to their direct reports; communication flowed in one direction. Today feedback is richer and more comprehensive, as it flows in all directions, offering us fresh perspectives and opportunities to cultivate true collaboration. But, as with all new methods, care must be taken to ensure the results are constructive–to all concerned.

If feedback is based on nefarious hidden agendas, it won't be worth the time taken to obtain it.

Receiving Feedback Internal Checklist

Considerations

Communication Options

Is this information directly from the source, or is this person a messenger?

→

If the person is a messenger, suggest that the "source" needs to problem solve directly with you.

What is the intent of the speaker?

→

If the intent of the discussion is unclear to you, ask the speaker to summarize his/her objectives.

Do you believe it's possible to have a productive, two-way discussion with the person?

Yes →

No →

Proceed.

Stop the conversation and explain that you'd like assurance that your point of view will be heard and respected.

What credibility does this person have from your perspective? Do you believe that their perspective is well developed? Do they practice the behaviors that are being discussed?

Yes →

No →

Proceed openly.

Proceed carefully. Remain as objective as possible and think about whether this information could help you in any possible way.

Organizational Surveys

Organizational surveys can take the pulse of an organization and provide global insights which can help organizations to benchmark levels of engagement. They can be a powerful tool for gathering information.

As a leader, however, you may find it difficult to hear what people have to say. You can benefit from surveys, but you have to keep your balance. There is a caveat here.

While these surveys are intended to open communication, their results may initially be unwieldy and even misleading. Bear in mind that the somewhat damning picture surveys may paint of your company is a natural expression of pent up frustration not specifically intended for any one leader. Don't lose your balance and feel like a **Karpman Drama Triangle** victim because of feedback that may be little more than a collective and cathartic rant.

A more effective approach to organizational surveys is to use them consistently and periodically, not only to open up communication in all directions, but also to gather information on engagement levels and other concrete indicators such as turnover, revenue, costs, and customer satisfaction.

Surveys can help leaders learn more about their company culture, so that they can prepare for more targeted and trenchant feedback later on.

But there is one more caution: The survey must be handled with care.

REALITY BITES

The Suspicious Survey

A client organization recently administered an Engagement Survey that failed to work as hoped. The employees were candid in their comments regarding the survey, but unfortunately not in their actual responses.

Their criticisms were two-fold: First of all, the employees believed that the questions were written in a way that forced a favorable response. Secondly, given that they had to identify their gender and location, there was additional reluctance to be candid.

The end result was nothing more than a stock answer: "Everything is fine." As George Carlin said, hair is fine, but people aren't fine.

And there is nothing fine about trying to get the truth from people whose trust you have not gained. Use a straightforward approach, get honest feedback, respond appropriately and you'll be on your way to authentic engagement.

For honesty and specificity, this next form of feedback can be a powerful motivator, for you as leader, or a time to practice **SNIP**.

360 Degree Assessments

The 360 Degree Assessment is a measure of what everyone you deal with thinks of your performance. This assessment, by virtue of its individual focus, has the potential to be painful and knock you off balance. The thoughts and feelings it gleans will be directed at you specifically. Best approached as a confidential process, its results can be rough going for you to hear.

On the other hand, and depending on how you receive its results, the 360 Degree Assessment can provide a wealth of information that can expand your awareness and improve your leadership abilities.

The best way to deal with this form of feedback is to review the report with a mentor or coach who is not your leader. This gives you some time to plan your actions before discussing them with your leader.

It is important not to fixate on the feedback of any one person. There will always be one or two people who take advantage of the veil of confidentiality to make scurrilous comments.

Rather, look for trends in the feedback. These will highlight both positive and negative patterns in your behavior, and help you keep on track while you keep your balance.

If all this talk of balance is a tad tiring, you may be relieved to know that the next form of feedback is colloquially know as a "sit-down."

One-on-Ones

An hour alone, on a regular basis, between you and your leader as well as each of your direct reports can be a powerful way to keep abreast of information and get to the heart of issues important to you as well as to the people on your team. You may think you don't have time for these sit-downs, but they offer rich rewards. One-on-One meetings help you develop respectful relationships, foster trust, and learn how to increase your engagement so that you can better engage your team.

REALITY BITES

The Power of a One-on-One

In 1991, after resigning as faculty and starting work with PepsiCo, I was introduced to the notion of the formal One-on-One meeting. My leader, Patrick McCann, scheduled an individual, private, confidential meeting with each one of his direct reports on a regular basis. Pat kept a file for these meetings and expected us to do the same. We updated each other, talked about projects and mutually offered both positive and constructive feedback. We both took the time to really listen to each other. Those meetings developed deep understanding, support, and respect. It also created a friendship that endures to this day.

Leaders routinely say that they don't have time for this kind of intense communication. What is more of a priority than ensuring that you, as well as your team, are going in the right direction with the right information and resources?

If your own leader does not initiate One-on-One discussions, ask him or her for an hour in order to provide update information. Hopefully the value of getting to know one another will be as evident to your leader as it is to you. By the same token, your direct reports will likely see the value in meeting with you regularly to discuss issues important to them.

People are more likely to follow you if they like you, and for someone to like you, they have to know you. Lead by example and offer your direct reports time to talk, and time for mutual understanding to grow. When they are in a position to do the same for their own direct reports, they will know the power of the One-on-One meeting from first hand experience.

Let's see how to apply the **Character Model** to the "sit-down."

One-on-One Engagement Conversations

Intention - Beliefs

Each person is responsible for the following:

- Knowing what will enhance their own level of engagement to the organization
- Providing the information to their leader
- Aligning their contribution to the organizational purpose

Thinking

- Knowing themselves in order to be honest and candid
- Considering the tools and resources required to do their job as effectively as possible
- Knowing what will add significance to their job

Feeling

- Handling emotion in order to have an open, candid discussion and develop a trusting relationship

Behavior

Both parties should do the following:

- Develop and respect norms for the conversation/process.
- Practice open listening.
- Hold the discussion confidential.
- Create solid action plans.
- Follow up to ensure momentum.

By taking these steps, you will have done your part to create a culture of engagement. Doing what you can to be engaged and engage the most people possible is what it's all about. So, let's meet the people in "town!"

Town Hall Meetings

This open forum allows you and your team to discuss the big issues affecting everyone. By first establishing ground rules for the meeting, you will create a climate in which some individuals will boldly express themselves. Others, reticent by nature, will still feel reluctant to open up. Interestingly, another effect, or benefit, will be that the group dynamics will be observable in the room. But, your balance will be required here, as camaraderie among members can be directed at you if everyone shares the same view on a hot issue.

At all times, in all encounters where viewpoints are shared, feedback offered, and issues aired, remember to keep **SNIP** at your hip, and you will be able to leverage your character and keep your balance.

Recap of Thoughts

In this chapter we have looked at the crucial importance of self-respect in making sure your organization is right for you, and whether or not you can establish and maintain your own engagement levels where you are currently working.

We saw how establishing your boundaries, resisting manipulation, and keeping your balance allows you to lead with self-respect, demonstrate your character, and benefit from the feedback you receive, even though some may be hard to hear.

You will need personal balance, as you will also find yourself in a position where you must give feedback, and you will need to be steady and ready for this key leadership responsibility. As you continue to assess your organization, you will be learning what it takes to respect and engage the people around you. At times you may still find yourself in the middle, but that doesn't mean you have to be a "monkey."

Putting It into Words and Actions

Being a *leader* means you have to respect yourself and find your path to engagement as well as help others find theirs. Below we look at the key measures and questions you can use to determine how to increase your engagement and maintain it.

Start with an assessment of your own engagement:

1. How Engaged Are You?

Complete the quiz at the following URL:
   www.centreforcharacterleadership.com/engagequiz.htm

Your Score_____

2. How Well Are You Keeping Your Balance?

Staying engaged means keeping your balance when faced with attempts to manipulate you.

Are you asking as much in terms of respect and commitment from your team as you ask of yourself?

How well are you practicing the concept of self-care?

When do you find yourself on the **Karpman Drama Triangle?**

What do you say or do to stay off the triangle?

3. Receiving Feedback

Keeping your balance is crucial when you receive feedback.

What is your reaction to feedback in general? From your own leader? From your peers? From your direct reports?

When does feedback sting the most?

How can you apply the Receiving Feedback Internal Checklist, which we introduced earlier in this chapter, to help you?

Consider how you can apply **SNIP** in order to help you manage your reactions to feedback effectively and how you can prepare yourself to receive it the future.

How can feedback help you in your intention to be a more engaging leader?

Putting It into Words: Receiving Feedback

Here are some ways you can respond effectively to feedback:

"Thank you for offering your perspective. This will help me become more effective at creating an engaging environment."

"Can you give me an example of when that happened? What do you recommend that I do in the future in a similar situation?"

"May I ask you to please offer feedback on what you have actually experienced? That has the most meaning for me."

 "May I ask you to let me know when you see me doing this more effectively in the future? That would be very encouraging and helpful."

"Let me know if you see me fall into this negative behavior again–I want to correct what I am doing."

Wanting to correct your behavior and improve your leadership is a clear example of leading through your authentic character. It also means you want to stay around, keep good employees and keep them energized.

When your character and self-respect are maintained you'll be in a much better position to engage others.

4. Holding One-on-One Engagement Conversations

Are you holding One-on-One Engagement Conversations with your leader?

How open and honest are these conversations?

What is the impact on your engagement level?

What will you do to ensure that you are respecting yourself in every way possible?

This last point on engagement brings us to our next chapter, Respect Others, in which we will get down to the business of how to practice the **Leadership Engagement Behaviors** with your team.

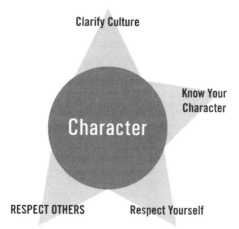

Clarify Culture

Know Your Character

Character

RESPECT OTHERS

Respect Yourself

The intention of Respect Others is to explore key insights in applying the **Leadership Engagement Behaviors.** The intention is also to highlight the importance of applying the **Character Model** in self-management, to allow you to practice engaging behaviors.

Respect Others is the grand thrust of authentic character engagement. It will show you how to retain and energize your team by demonstrating leadership behaviors that work.

Intentional Acts of Character
The Precarious Kitchen: Chill the Worry and Warm the Heart

Brenda had worked for a restaurant company for fifteen years, having started out as a helper in the kitchen before working her way up to the position of cook. She was about thirty-five years old when she fell ill and required surgery to remove her gall bladder. As the company offered no sick benefits, not unlike many other service organizations, she knew that her time off would mean she would receive no money except for what she could receive through government benefits. Brenda, a single mom, was worried about rent, food, and her child. One of the staff at her restaurant saw how dire the situation was for her and started a fund to raise money to support their cook, whom other employees had long regarded as a vital ingredient of the restaurant. The managers and hourly workers, most receiving minimum wage themselves, pitched in, raising a few thousand dollars to help Brenda, who recuperated from her surgery knowing her team members cared about her well-being as much as her delicious lunch specials.

Respect Others

The world is moved along, not only by the mighty shoves of its heroes,
but also by the aggregate of the tiny pushes of each honest worker.

Helen Keller

This chapter is longer than the others, and for good reason. Having explored all the layers of your unique character, it's time to get to the heart of the matter, the thrust of the book–the connection between character, respecting others, and behavior that engages people.

The **Leadership Engagement Behaviors** may appear simple, even obvious, but applying them on a consistent basis is not an easy fix. Engaging and respecting your team can be as difficult to master as the workplace is demanding.

How do you put your authentic character to work? What does it take? It takes your choice. In all cases engaging others requires intention, discipline, and steady focus; requires the same high level of respect for others that you have for yourself.

Practice the Leadership Engagement Behaviors	
1.	Treat people in a consistently civil manner.
2.	Tell the truth.
3.	Listen openly with empathy.
4.	Conduct yourself in an ethical manner.
5.	Create an atmosphere of camaraderie.
6.	Provide autonomy to make decisions.
7.	Articulate clear, measurable, achievable performance expectations.
8.	Recognize contributions frequently, specifically and personally.
9.	Address performance gaps in a timely, private, problem solving manner.
10.	Provide opportunities for people to find challenge and significance in their work.
11.	Ensure training and learning opportunities are available.
12.	Provide proper tools and resources.

This list is your set of behavioral tools for enhancing your leadership and improving the performance of your workplace–for realizing your character potential. Yes, it takes work, but work in the right direction is better than futility, any day.

So, let's get to it.

1. Treat People in a Consistently Civil Manner

Character Connection

There are those who scoff at the very idea that everyone deserves to be treated with respect, calling the expectation unreasonable. Respect, they say, is earned, not given freely. True, no one can demand your respect; nor can you demand that someone respect you.

What is reasonable is to expect that you are treated and treat every person civilly. Respect comes in time. Civility, on the other hand, is about common human decency, and it is the minimum requirement in any interaction, no matter what the subject matter. It's a beginning to engagement, the first step in making your character connection, and it begins, as always, at the core.

Your Character–Civility

Intentions

Beliefs

- All people are equal; we are just doing different jobs.
- There are at least two sides to every situation.
- It is important to care about the well-being of every person.
- You are all unique and bring special talents and gifts to the workplace.
- It is important to know and leverage your own unique gifts as well as those of others in the workplace.
- You have your own unique way of hearing, processing and responding to information.

Goals

- Understand all the facts and the perspectives of a situation before drawing a conclusion.
- Treat every person, in every conversation, civilly.

Thoughts

- Gather facts, information and perspectives in an open-minded, problem-solving manner.
- Don't presume to know what a person thinks, feels, or is trying to say.

Feelings

- Identify and manage your feelings of delight, pride, satisfaction, frustration, anger, etc., in any conversation.
- Adjust your behavior when you are observing feelings of excitement, enthusiasm, anger, disappointment, frustration etc., in another person.

Civilized Behavior

C	Care
I	Involve
V	Value
I	Inform
L	Listen

Care

- Demonstrate that you want the person to be successful.
- Show that they are capable of doing the job.
- Never humiliate, shame, attack, put down or degrade anyone.

Involve

- Balance asking and telling.
- Involve people in decisions that impact them.

Value

- Value their input.
- When you ask their opinion, offer feedback.

Inform

- Explain your performance expectations.
- Offer feedback, both positive and constructive.

Listen

- Listen fully and openly, without interruption.
- Test both your understanding and their understanding of important messages.

Civility involves recognizing the common humanity in all of us. Unfortunately, bad behavior is also a trait we all share, at least some of the time. However, dealing with incivility properly is not a common enough trait among leaders.

Civility When the Going Gets Rough

Treating people with civility doesn't mean you are perpetually sweet, acquiescent or passive. Character behavior means that you do what is appropriate for the situation in a civilized, fair manner.

If someone has been abusive to a colleague, address the offending person assertively and firmly, but listen to their perspective to get the whole story. At the end of the conversation you may decide to suspend the person or terminate their employment. But at no time should you treat the person as they have treated your colleague. You have a choice.

The workplace may be filled with huffing, puffing, and back-stabbing, but whose behavior do you want to model? It's your character. Do the right thing–treat people civilly.

Civil behavior is the right thing for many reasons. Not only does it make you and others feel better, but civility helps people work better together, improving performance and your organization's bottom line.

According to a study conducted by Public Virtues in 2000, more than 79 percent of workers have seen incivility in the workplace, and as many as 50 percent have had the urge to be uncivil at work. Also, more than 23 percent have permanently left their place of work due to incivility, and 56 percent of respondents felt that organizations lose money because of incivility.[1]

We will take a much closer look at civility, or the lack thereof, in our next chapter, Harness Conflict. For now, let's look at the **Leadership Engagement Behavior** which, along with respect, underpins trust.

2. Tell the Truth

It is the duty of men to judge men only by their actions. Our faculties furnish us with no means of arriving at the motive, the character, the secret self. We call the tree good from its fruits, and the man, from his works.

Ralph Waldo Emerson

Character Connection

It takes courage to tell the truth, because not everyone will appreciate your perspective, boundaries, and insights. As an organizational leader you are accountable to speak up–to your own leader, your peers, and your direct reports. Though "yes" people may believe they are being politically savvy, what they are really doing is shirking responsibility.

Managers often gossip about the shortcomings of an employee who has yet to hear a word about what others have been saying in their absence. The accused person often senses something is amiss, and yet they have not had the opportunity to move in the right direction. Not surprisingly, an individual alienated is an individual disengaged.

Why do leaders hesitate to tell their team members the truth? Mostly out of fear of the following:

- A reaction which may lead to conflict
- Damaging the relationship
- Hurting the person's feelings
- Embarrassing the person
- Being accused of being a poor leader
- Looking foolish
- Finding out something they don't know or don't want to know
- The team's response

Fear not. Henry David Thoreau wrote, "We sit as many risks as we run." My own experiences bear this out. I have found that when I stand up and confront my fears they become much less daunting and far more manageable. When approached and overcome with courage, fear gives us opportunities to make true progress, from the inside out.

Character behavior challenges you to wrestle fear to the ground and tell the truth. Keep **SNIP** in your hip pocket. This handy tool will help you master your emotions and align your behavior with your intentions. Not only will you avoid stressful disharmony, but you will be one situation, one person closer to engaging your team.

Honesty starts with you.

Pronouns Are Important

Speaking from the *I* is one of the most powerful ways to tell the truth.

Yes, there is no *I* in team, which is important to remember when you are describing team accomplishments. In such cases, certainly use *you* and *we*.

When you are offering your opinion, especially in potentially volatile situations, speak for yourself "*I* can contribute more to our meetings when *I* have an agenda a couple of days in advance" will go over better than "you didn't send the agenda out ahead of time."

Or, as another example, it is better to say "*I* am unclear about how to approach this task" rather than "you didn't explain this well enough."

Character Leaders Judge Performance, Not People

The ability to distinguish between a person and their behavior is how engaging, caring leaders get the best results. Instead of calling a person "lazy, ineffective or loser," say, "He has missed three assignment deadlines." This helps avoid negative images in the workplace and sets the stage for constructive performance discussions down the road.

3. Listen Openly with Empathy

Character Connection

Listening is difficult. Today the workplace is so busy there never seems to be enough time even for essential tasks. So, hearing what people are truly saying can be a challenge. Also consider that you may not like their point of view. You may be annoyed that they have omitted or even twisted facts in an attempt to manipulate you. Ironically, you may be frustrated that the other person can't hear what you're saying. This is common, and very human. But listening is about them. You matter here in that your intention is to listen and gather information. But they matter when they are speaking, so listen fully, *with empathy*.

Listen, Acknowledge, and Ask is a model for effective listening with empathy at the heart of the three step process.

Listen–Acknowledge–Ask

LISTEN ACKNOWLEDGE ASK

Listen

Listen and truly hear what is being said

- Clear your mind of internal noise, and focus.
- Put yourself in the other person's shoes and consider their perspective before, during, and after the conversation.
- Listen openly and observe tone of voice and body language, to understand what the person is truly trying to convey. It is just as important that you hear what the person isn't vocalizing.

Acknowledge

Don't make assumptions about motives, thoughts, or feelings

- Don't judge. Keep your mind open regarding thoughts, feelings, and motives. Their perspective is valid to them.
- Don't interrupt, debate, deny, or mock the person.
- Acknowledge what the person is saying. Repeat it back to them to test your understanding of their message.
- Connect to the person through empathy. Sincerely acknowledging the emotion reassures the person that you understand on two levels, message and emotion.

Putting It into Words: Acknowledge

"I understand that you are *angry*. Let's work together to find a solution so this doesn't happen again."

"I hear your *disappointment;* let's find a way so this is never repeated."

"Your *enthusiasm* is contagious. Congratulations on your success."

"I see that you are *frustrated* with the current situation. Let's brainstorm some solutions."

"It appears that you are *uneasy* in our team meetings. That is an *uncomfortable* position to be in."

Ask

Clarify the message with open-ended questions

- Ask questions beginning with words like *who, what, where, when, how, and why* rather than questions requiring a yes or no answer: "What was effective and what needs to be improved in our meetings?" versus "Was the meeting effective?"
- A word to the *why*. Asking people to explain their choices may put them on the defensive. It is often more constructive to ask something like: "What led you to make that decision?"
- Don't offer solutions. Rather than jumping in with advice, ask the person for their thoughts about how to solve the issue, so that the solution will be *theirs,* not yours.

Empathy means hearing, not agreeing

Remember, empathizing with someone doesn't mean that you agree; it means you hear and understand their perspective. If you work hard to understand a person they will likely try to understand you.

Many a manager has asked: "Why on earth do I have to understand my employees?" Some believe that emotion doesn't belong in the workplace, that emotion can only cloud our judgment and lead us to the wrong decisions.

The need to feel understood is fundamental. That it ranks high on the hierarchy of human needs is, well, understandable.[2] Empathy allows us to be aware of and sensitive to the feelings, thoughts, and experiences of others without actually sharing the feelings or emotions of another.[3] This is quite a powerful human faculty when you think about it.

Empathy creates mutual understanding–a foundation for collaboration.

Given that work is about collaborating with others, empathy, rather than muddying the waters, helps us to clarify situations, facilitate solutions, and lead more effectively, engagingly, and with character.

REALITY BITES

Roots of Empathy

Roots of Empathy (ROE) is a Toronto-based program which aims to teach emotional literacy, cultivate empathy, and develop character in children.

Founded by Mary Gordon and supported by educators, politicians, and celebrities, ROE reaches children of all ages across Canada, Australia, New Zealand, and the United States, teaching the values of social awareness like empathy, respect, and inclusion.

At the heart of the program are a neighbourhood infant and parent who visit the classroom every three weeks over the school year. A trained ROE Instructor coaches students to observe the baby's development and to label the baby's feelings. In this experiential learning, the baby is the "Teacher" and a lever, which the instructor uses to help children identify and reflect on their own feelings and the feelings of others. This "emotional literacy" taught in the program lays the foundation for more safe and caring classrooms, where children are the "Changers." They are more competent in understanding their own feelings and the feelings of others (empathy) and are therefore less likely to physically, psychologically and emotionally hurt each other through bullying and other cruelties. In the ROE program children learn how to challenge cruelty and injustice. Messages of social inclusion and activities that are consensus building contribute to a culture of caring that changes the tone of the classroom. The ROE Instructor also visits before and after each family visit to prepare and reinforce teachings using a specialized lesson plan for each visit. Research results from national and international evaluations of ROE indicate significant reductions in aggression and increases in pro-social behaviour.[4]

Roots of Empathy, the success of which has resulted in Ms. Gordon's investiture to the Order of Canada, has shown it can reduce the levels of aggression and violence in children.

Clearly, there are many people in many countries who value what Ms. Gordon is doing and feel enough is enough: that it is time to proactively create societies where decency and character are the norm. We will return to the subject of bad behavior in chapter six, Harness Conflict.

For now, it may be helpful to remember that children and adults can learn character, but intentionality and responsibility starts with adults, with all of us.

4. Conduct Yourself in an Ethical Manner

Character Connection

Many of us have been presented with company booklets entitled "Code of Conduct." But how often have they helped us understand our true intentions and how we define success? When success is defined as power over people, financial gain, and the trappings of privilege, then people may be tempted to behave unethically. On the other hand, if you define success as consistently behaving in a fair, honorable and responsible manner, then your conduct will be ethical, on the path of engagement. Ironically, ethical organizations more fully engage their people and produce results.

Authentically Ethical

An authentic leader strives to behave ethically because it is the right thing to do, not just because it will yield better bottom line results. This means admitting mistakes without hedging, fudging, or ducking.

You Are a Role Model

As soon as you are an "official" leader in your organization, you will be watched carefully. People will follow your example, and you can influence the culture of the organization and how people judge it. You don't have to be perfect, but you do have an additional responsibility of managing yourself from the inside out. So, you have to behave in an intentional, appropriate, aligned manner.

The Stakes Have Risen

Not that many years ago the statement "it is a business decision" meant that any decision that reaped profit was deemed acceptable. Today life is not that simple. We have watched in horror as prominent business leaders are branded criminals. We face unfathomable environmental consequences if we don't act more responsibly towards our planet. And conflict in the workplace can mean that people die. So leaders have an inescapable responsibility to ensure that they are paying attention and facing the tough challenges that have inestimable consequences.

5. Create an Atmosphere of Camaraderie and Fun

Laughter is the closest distance between two people.

Victor Borge

Character Connection

This is serious: The more people laugh and enjoy the workplace, the better the results. Believe it. Laughter is good for us, both mentally and physically.

To take Borge's quotation further, laughter can bring an entire group together, relieving common tensions and galvanizing shared purposes.

A workplace is a community of people. As humans, we need to feel that we belong in order to feel safe. And we create a sense of belonging by connecting with each other through emotions and laughter.

Feeling we belong can also sway our decision to stay. Lisa Belkin, a journalist with the New York Times, cited research by Ipsos that found that those whose managers have a good sense of humor are more likely to stick around than those whose managers lack a sense of humor.[5]

Have Fun–Without Risk

I'm not proposing your team join hands and sing "Kumbaya." Nor am I suggesting beer and wings every day after work. Either extreme is not without its own risks, foreseeable and otherwise. What's important is that people have opportunities to know each other beyond email.

I know from my coaching work that many people want to feel part of the team as well as create their own team, but are unsure how to go about it.

Pot luck lunches, volunteer projects for various causes, and informal celebrations are just some of the ways people can connect and feel part of a team. Some organizations hold fun competitions similar to The Amazing Race, or hockey games, or Scrabble tournaments.

However you go about it, the foundation of the team is to set a standard for highly functioning behavior, which is your responsibility. So have fun with it!

Humor at the Right Time

It is a gift to be able to crack a joke at the right time. Laughter diffuses tension and helps us focus on solutions rather than whatever caused the tension in the first place. It is social music, the very sound of civility at its best. While not all of us are born with the wit of Oscar Wilde, we can as leaders keep an eye (and ear) out for tense moments.

If you have it in you to make people laugh, let it out. It'll help. And even if *bon mots* are not your forte, by creating a culture of levity, you can encourage others to be funny. When good feelings are circulating among the employees, you know you are doing the right things to retain and energize your team.

It's a Virtual World

We work in a very different way than we did twenty-five years ago. The norm was to commute to a central location where we would socialize during breaks or lunch. Today many of us work from remote locations–home office, a cottage, a ski lodge, a boat traveling the canals of Europe, or some combination thereof. Internet access and telephone service make it possible to be part of a team wherever we are. But while technology continues to change, life continues to be enriched by social contact. So, by encouraging your team members to meet face-to-face you will get the best from them when they are working on their own.

6. Support Autonomy to Make Decisions

Treat people as if they were what they ought to be, and you help them become what they are capable of becoming.

Johann W. von Goethe

Character Connection

It can be frightening to let people make their own decisions. For one thing, they might do things their own way. The good news is that if you give people autonomy, they likely *will* do things their own way. Hey, if you didn't hire corporate clones in the first place, why would you expect your team members to go about things in the same manner?

Your job as leader is to clarify direction, provide guiding parameters, and then support people in their roles. While the workplace is not a free-for-all, the right level of risk, in alignment with your company culture, will produce soaring results.

Support Mistakes

Mistakes allow us to learn. It's evolutionary. Though making the same mistakes over and over is bad, fear of trying and failing should not rule the workplace. You work with adults, so respect them as such. Handle mistakes privately and with civility. Support autonomy, respond appropriately to mistakes and you will engage your way right through one of the most common fears in the workplace.

As one client declared, "I feel like the coach and the head cheerleader wrapped into one!"

Let's Hear It for the Coach!

With Lois Tori

As a leader one of the best ways that you can engage your employees in the development process is to be their coach.

You may have read a lot about coaching, as it has quickly become one of the most critical processes for enhancing employee development in today's competitive organizations.

So what is coaching? The International Coaching Federation defines coaching as:

> "Coaching is partnering with clients in a thought-provoking and creative process that inspires them to maximize their personal and professional potential.
>
> Coaching is an ongoing relationship which focuses on clients taking action toward the realization of their visions, goals or desires. Coaching uses a process of inquiry and personal discovery to build the client's level of awareness and responsibility and provides the client with structure, support and feedback. The coaching process helps clients both define and achieve professional and personal goals faster and with more ease than would be possible otherwise."[6]

The overall purpose of coaching is to help others learn, develop, adapt, and grow. It can be a very engaging and empowering process for both the leader and the employee.

Though it is your employee's decision to pursue personal development, it is your role, as the coach, to help the person begin the journey and to support him or her along the way.

Coaching has often been viewed as a strategy just for dealing with employee performance problems. From that viewpoint it doesn't seem very different from corrective feedback. Coaching for continuous improvement, engagement, or excellence is very different from the conversation that takes place when there is a gap between actual and expected performance. To be successful, coaches must understand this difference and act accordingly.

In both cases good coaches focus on the person before focusing on the performance. By offering support, leaders foster the employee's confidence in his or her own abilities, helping the person develop from the inside out.

However, being supportive doesn't mean being passive, as you will often be required to challenge your direct report to face alternative perspectives. The key is to be honest and respectful, and to let the person know you believe in their ability to achieve their goals. It is your job to hold your employee accountable to commitments. Remember, you are only responsible for your part of the coaching partnership. You're there to listen, talk, and sometimes provide a different perspective.

Think of the sports you've played. Did the coach run the field or skate the ice for you? Similarly, you can't learn or achieve for your employees.

Clarify who owns what of the work.

The real success of coaching is realized when a foundation of mutual trust and respect grows, allowing you to create a partnership that engages your employee and helps him or her to develop, as you will see in the following **Reality Bite**.

REALITY BITES

Impact and Influence: A Coaching Success Story

During my time in various leadership roles at Royal Bank Canada, I used the coaching approach with my direct reports to help them rise to their potential. Every week I would set aside time for coaching. The topic was always their choice and it ranged from daily work issues to how they could achieve their career goals.

This process was particularly rewarding as my direct reports developed their own plans to tackle issues and develop competencies. Their plans were often much better than any advice I could have given them, and their commitment level to follow through was remarkably high.

In other words, they were fully engaged!

I recall working with a young leader who was in his first leadership role as a branch manager. He had settled into the role and wanted to start contributing more to the management team. Though he had some great ideas, they were often rejected by the more senior members of the team, who seemed to think that his inexperience precluded his ability to think and contribute.

When I arranged a coaching session with him, he chose to work on the above issue. I believed that his ideas were valuable. I reassured him that he had the potential to be a very good leader and that I would support him in any way I could.

Through the session we looked at his competency level for "impact and influence." He felt there was an opportunity to structure an action plan to improve. He got to work.

After doing research on suggested activities, he decided one of his actions would be to gather support for his ideas from several of his colleagues before making the suggestion to the entire team. This worked so well that he applied the same action plan to his various activities outside of work. Because the action plan was his own he was committed to following through, which he did, coming through with flying colors. Not only did he successfully increase his level of competency, but his ideas and efforts at the management team level contributed to everyone's success, including my own.

Lois Tori

As you can see, the value of coaching for engagement can be seen, felt, and measured across the organization. If you don't feel like shouting, "Hip, hip, hooray!" then put your energy and enthusiasm into actions.

Coach your team, engage your team, and everyone wins.

7. Articulate Clear, Measurable, Achievable Performance Expectations

Character Connection

You have hired intelligent adults who can think for themselves but that doesn't mean they can read minds. As human beings we need the security of knowing what is expected of us. Your team needs clarity, not micromanaging, in order to thrive. Clear expectations create a sense of safety and commitment in your team members. People want to know how to behave at dinner parties–why not in the workplace?

As a leader, you have to clarify for your employees what is expected of them and why. When you articulate performance expectations you will not only make it possible for the feedback process to work later on, but you will also help your employees understand how their performance affects the entire organization.

Talking Behaviors

In Clarify the Culture, we discussed the importance of creating and maintaining a culture in which all employees understand expected behaviors. Focusing on what character means to your organization and how behavior will be evaluated along with other performance measures will allow your team members to see how their character can contribute to the culture and goals of entire organization. If they can't see it, they can't achieve it.

Start Talking Behaviors Early

Clarify performance expectations the moment a person starts the job, when a new task or project is outlined, or when objectives change. Measurable, either qualitatively or quantitatively, performance expectations should be followed up with feedback, both positive and developmental.

Keep Talking Behaviors

One of the most powerful leadership techniques is to hold the aforementioned regular One-on-One conversations, every two to three weeks. As these discussions are two-way in nature, they offer each of you a tremendous opportunity to share and receive important information; and you, as leader, to provide feedback and ensure open communication. You may think you are too busy for this. But ask yourself: What is more important than keeping your team members updated, aligned, and focused?

REALITY BITES

Specialized Talent, Common Goals, Shared Direction

Everyone needs some sort of direction if they wish to move forward. This sounds simple, but for leaders in information-based organizations, the challenge lies in knowing how much direction to give highly skilled individuals, or specialists.

Peter F. Drucker commented on this very challenge back in 1998, when we were in the midst of great technological upheaval in the workplace.

In *The Coming of the New Organizations* in the Harvard Business Review, Drucker wrote that just because specialists in information-based organizations can't be told how to do their jobs, they still need a few clear and common objectives that can be translated into particular actions.

In order to proceed with their work effectively, specialists must understand what management expects of every team and of the entire organization, and what they expect of each player to meet overall expectations.

In addition to clear and simple expectations, everyone in an information – based organization must regularly consider the information that they need to contribute to the achievement of organizational goals.[7]

8. Recognize Contributions Frequently, Specifically and Personally

Catch people doing something right.

Ken Blanchard

Character Connection

Feeling valued is a significant human need. Recognition energizes, inspiring confidence and risk taking. When people know the value and positive impact of their actions, they move forward with certainty and courage.

And yet in the past fifteen years of holding workshops, as few as five people have indicated to me that they are richly recognized for their contributions at work. Leaders are missing some key opportunities to engage.

There are many books about the ways to recognize employees. Gifts, rewards and incentives are good, but nothing replaces the feeling of being sincerely appreciated by the people around you, especially by your leader.

So why aren't leaders offering more positive reinforcement? Isn't it easy to say nice things? Not always.

The many reasons for leaders' reticence are spread throughout the **Character Model**.

The Character Model–Reactive Behavior

Intentions

- I only give feedback when it is truly exceptional. I pay people to do their job.

Thoughts

- I don't have time to notice that level of detail.
- I don't receive positive feedback myself, so why should I offer it?

Feelings

- I'm not sure how the person will react, or that they will ask me for something as a result. I am concerned about what other people will say.
- I feel undervalued.

Behavior

- I'm not sure how to actually say it without sounding odd.
- It isn't my nature to be so effusive. People know what I think. I don't think people like hearing that kind of thing. I prefer to make a note on their performance review.
- I will offer recognition when I feel recognized.

But, for every wrong behavior there is a right behavior . . .

The Character Model–Proactive Behavior

Intentions

Beliefs

- People repeat behavior that is recognized.
- Positive reinforcement encourages people to do their best.
- The more we believe that we are valued by our leader, the easier it is to hear the constructive feedback.
- I must truly value what I am recognizing or it's an insincere gesture.
- The more specific my feedback, the more powerful.
- Timing is important: the more immediate, the more effective.

Goals

- It's a priority to notice and recognize the positive contribution of each person in my team.

Thoughts

- I notice what each person is doing and how they are doing it, and consider the impact their actions are having on the team.
- I notice reactions to positive feedback, and think about how to offer this information in the most appropriate manner for each person. I think about how to deliver the message.

- I know that this is the right thing to do. Perhaps if my leader notices the improvement he or she will start being more generous with their positive feedback.

Feelings

- I discipline myself to work through my discomfort when offering praise. I pay attention to my reactions, to ensure I express myself as I intend.
- I find the generosity and fairness to offer positive feedback even when I am discouraged and disappointed by my own situation.
- I pay attention to the other person's emotions, adjusting my approach accordingly. If they appear embarrassed I finish the conversation quickly, or ask if they would like to reschedule.

Behavior

Positive Feedback - O.I.–Observation, Impact

Observation	Impact
Positive Feedback	
"I noticed you submitted the report before the due date."	*"Thanks, that makes it easier to review and make any changes before we go to print. Much appreciated."*

A simple format for offering feedback is to state your observation and describe the impact (**O.I.**):

"I noticed you submitted the report before the due date. (observation) Thanks, that makes it easier to review and make any changes before we go to print. (impact) Much appreciated."

By practicing your delivery using this format, you can prepare for a conversation ahead of time. The beauty of **O.I.** lies in its simple cause-and-effect logic. Not only can it minimize emotional discomfort, yours and theirs, but it can engage even the most modest of people.

Be ready for the person to respond and further discuss the what, how and why. Two-way understanding is always a good thing.

9. Address Performance Gaps in a Timely, Private, Problem Solving Manner

Character Connection

The flipside of offering positive feedback is confronting inappropriate behavior. As this is a non-negotiable part of your job, it is not only potentially unpleasant but something you have to deal with. First, let's look at the many reasons *not* to do the right thing.

The Character Model–Reactive Behavior

Intentions

- I believe it will hurt the feelings of the other person.
- It isn't worth the aggravation or paperwork.
- It has gone on for a long time, so I will let it go.

Thoughts

- It will go away on its own.
- I will transfer out of this job and someone else will deal with it.
- I don't know how to solve this.
- I don't want to be seen as leader who causes trouble.
- Will this prolonged action block me from getting another job?
- My boss isn't going to appreciate another problem landing on her desk.
- I don't want to hear accusations regarding my performance as leader.

Feelings

You fear the following:

- Conflict with that person, or an emotional reaction
- Reaction of co-workers
- Grievances
- A prolonged, uncomfortable process
- The reaction of your boss
- Negative impact on your career

Behaviors

- I don't complete the documentation required.
- I don't know how to confront this to get the result I want.
- I prefer to write them an email than say it face to face.
- Doing nothing and disengaging the "good" workers.

REALITY BITES

The Strain Caused by Elaine

Elaine was a government employee, a civil servant in a unionized job, with a work schedule of 37.5 hours per week and generous vacation time. Yet, despite her relatively relaxed work environment, her performance was a 52/48 split: 52 percent of the time she was barely meeting performance expectations, and 48 percent of the time she was behind or deficient in her workload.

Over the years her supervisors had rated Elaine's performance as "acceptable." Supervisors tended to rotate in that department, so there was a general reluctance to confront performance issues, particularly with employees who would resist the feedback and cause increased documentation, tension within the team, and general heartache.

Elaine's work was becoming increasingly worrisome. Complaints were piling up, documentation was incomplete, and team members, having to assume her workload during her frequent absences, were stressed out.

Her leader, Ann, documented the facts and confronted Elaine, whose reaction was one of utter surprise. No one had ever challenged her or pointed out performance gaps. Her defense was that she was behind due to her lengthy vacations and sick days.

Elaine contacted her union representative who, in her opinion, didn't properly defend her. She visited her doctor and was granted an extended stress leave, at full pay!

During that time, Elaine contacted her teammates to complain about the unfair actions of their leader. The leader couldn't discuss the case for ethical reasons.

Eventually she was censured. The performance information stayed in her file.

Ann says that leaders who ignore performance issues are doing a disservice to all concerned.

Poor performance gaps, left unaddressed, can poison an entire team. Though avoidance is tempting and easier in the short run, running and hiding from a problem will never make it go away. As a leader, you have to respect the entire team.

In such cases there is only one direction for the authentically engaging leader.

The Character Model–Proactive Behavior

Developmental Conversations - O.I.Q.A.

Here is a simple way to deal with that "dreaded" discussion.

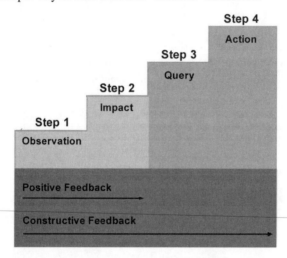

Observation, Impact, Query, Action (O.I.Q.A.):

Leader: I noticed that you were very quiet during the meeting this morning. *(Observation)*

I'm not sure whether the meeting was relevant/informative for you or not. The rest of us were making decisions without your input. (Impact)

What was happening? (Query)

Tony: I had a lot going on and didn't know what we were going to discuss.

(Here you can apply **Listen, Acknowledge, and Ask**)

Leader: So, you were a bit stressed with everything you had to get done and didn't receive the agenda, is that what you are saying?(Listen/Acknowledge)

Tony: That is about it.

Leader: Is there anything else I should know about this? (Ask)

Tony: Well, I think we go off on tangents and lose time.

Leader: Ok, thanks for telling me. What do you see as our options? (Listen Openly)

Tony: Well, I would like to see the agenda prior to the meeting and with timelines for each item.

Leader: Fair enough, if I commit to get a detailed agenda to you prior to the meeting, what is your commitment? (Query)

Tony: I will be able to participate if I have the agenda. (response)

Leader: So, you are saying that if you receive the agenda ahead of the meeting your participation will be more robust. Is that correct? (Action/Confirmation)

Tony: Yes, that is my commitment. (response)

Leader: Great, thank you. I appreciate the conversation.

The **O.I.Q.A.** process will help you simplify and focus on the matter at hand: addressing performance problems of the team member in front of you. The key here is to be fair and forthright. Because in all likelihood, the person in question has been the subject of commentary–some true, some false. Sitting down to talk will give both of you an opportunity to clear the air, the other person information to improve their behavior, and you a chance to increase engagement and trust. It depends on how the conversation goes–which direction is chosen.

REALITY BITES

Enter the Dragon: Struggling with Constructive Feedback

Honesty is cited as one of the **Leadership Engagement Behaviors.** Yet, when there is a gap between expected and actual performance, leaders often freeze. Talking about the gap can be as painful as it is to take action to bridge it.

As Patricia from chapter one says, "I know that I range from yelling at the person to saying nothing and being totally ticked off with them. I don't know how to say it the 'right way.'"

She isn't the only person to feel the jolting kick of the fight-or-flight response in situations of disapproval or disappointment. When leaders feel this way, conversations have the potential for conflict. The person in question might not like being told that improvement is required.

Yes, "stars," be they athletes or actors, pay boatloads of money to coaches to help them improve. But that is different–they request that feedback.

When feedback is unsolicited we risk offending people–deeply. So, what about this? It's your responsibility to keep your team members on track. How do you do this in a way that doesn't de-motivate them? To do so would, ironically, defeat the purpose of offering constructive feedback in the first place.

What if you make a pact with your direct reports to offer them your perspective on how they can improve their performance in a regular fashion? One highly effective approach is to first point out, during your One-on-One conversations, what they are truly, legitimately doing well and then focus on one or two suggestions for improvement.

After all, it's their responsibility to seek engagement and improvement (as it is yours), so that they can meet performance targets set through feedback and discussions.

However, if they turn you down you have trouble, because it's your responsibility to make sure they're on track.

But be prepared: Feedback discussions pivot on a moment, which can either go well or . . . not so well. You may find yourself at 'Y' in the road.

MAGIC MOMENT

Engage or Enrage in the Blink of a 'Y'

Trust and communication are related. Yes, trust can grow over time, but there is a basic level of trust required in every encounter we face; that is, if we want to move forward. Communication can be either a one-off act or the start of a healthy connection between parties.

In tough conversations there is often a critical 'Y' in which the outcome will be either positive or negative, and it has a lot to do with the level of trust and understanding between the parties at that moment in time.

When the two people are truly working to understand each other they achieve resonance (creating a sense of connection), which moves the conversation, and the relationship, in the right direction. But when egos clash or perspectives are at odds, dissonance and distrust can occur, breaking the connection and moving conversation in the wrong direction.

The negative turn on the "Y" often happens so fast that it catches both parties off guard. This typically occurs when one person touches on something sensitive, reveals a perspective based on unknown or inaccurate facts, or launches into an accusation.

If the receiver becomes irate, defends a position, or attacks back, the negative road has been chosen–connection is lost, and the chance to engage the person may be gone. You've stumbled at the 'Y' in the road.

However, if the receiver has the ability to remain calm, apply **SNIP** and **Listen, Acknowledge, and Ask,** then the two of you have a chance to turn the conversation in the positive direction, and achieve the results you intended to achieve–engagement.

However, what about poor performance that can't be turned around?

REALITY BITES

Poor Performers: Are We Saying Hello or Goodbye?

It happens. You take over a new area of the organization, only to find that someone (or perhaps several people) who has languished in his job. Whether he's doing the wrong kind of work or simply tired of his position, the challenge you face is how to handle the situation.

Start with the truth. This is no time to equivocate. As we've seen, poor performers can affect the morale of others, which has an impact on team engagement and results, for which you were hired to be accountable. Clarify performance expectations, just as you would with a new recruit, and then ask him to participate in the goal setting, monitoring, support requirement, and follow-up communication.

There is a positive possibility here, an opportunity to start afresh. If he chooses to meet expectations, terrific–celebrate! You're a step closer to engagement. But if he chooses not to improve and meet performance expectations, respect his choice, and then let him go. It's fair to the team, to you, and even to him.

Time is valuable. Someone not doing a fair day's work is not an option, and a leader of character will not tolerate it. Disengagement and wasted opportunities are no good for anyone.

So when a situation like this does happen, act quickly, knowing you've done the right thing–whichever direction the outcome takes.

You and your team will need to handle the momentary challenges in order to take on the larger, long-term ones, finding greater meaning and opportunities in their work.

10. Provide Opportunities for People to Find Challenge and Significance in Their Work

Character Connection

We human beings need to feel that there's a purpose to our lives, that what we do matters to those around us and will contribute to our own legacy as well as our workplace and community. The need to connect to the world from the inside out is profoundly important.

Line of Sight

Some jobs are regarded as less important than others. People may even dismiss their own jobs as meaningless. Part of your responsibility as an engaging leader is to help each person on your team understand how their job contributes to the overall purpose of the organization.

There may be more to "significance" than just the company's bottom line.

REALITY BITES

Community Impact

More and more companies, from banks to hi-tech firms, are getting involved in volunteer and charitable work, as leaders and employees are seeing their purpose within the community in a new way.

While the positive impact on the community is obvious, the benefits to organizations range from positive reputation to increased market share to increased trust among investors.

Perhaps the most profound impact volunteering has on an organization is in the area of employee satisfaction and engagement.

Anthony Meehan, publisher of Canada's Top 100 Employers, stated that "since the book's first edition in 1992 a strong correlation has been observed between charitable work and how an employer treats its own employees. Employers who take a broader view of their community responsibilities, it turns out, are almost always better places to work."[8]

By seeing leadership and employee roles in a broader light, we can create organizational cultures with broader scope.

Challenge People to Have Impact

During your One-on-One meetings ask "what can we do to provide more challenge for you?" or "what would it require for you to feel that your role in this organization is as significant as possible for you?"

Mind you, a sense of purpose in our work can seem like a frustrating, unrealizable dream if we don't have the right opportunities to learn or the right tools to fulfill our purpose by bringing our goals to fruition.

As a leader, you need to equip your team members.

11. Ensure Training and Learning Opportunities Are Available

Character Connection

Remember the days of carbon copies? If not, then you are living proof of the speed at which technology is driving change. We have gone from photocopies to floppy disks to CD-ROMs to memory sticks in less than a generation. Technology is changing all facets of life, allowing us to learn more about ourselves and how we think. Long gone are the days when parents and children learned the same stuff. Today's workplace requires leaders of courage and perseverance, who will embrace change and engage their teams with opportunities to learn and grow.

Learning at Work

Training programs aren't the only ways to learn. The job itself is an arena for learning and developing skills sets. Present the people on your team with new projects and challenges–opportunities to stretch their knowledge, skill set, and confidence. Keep in mind, however, that what engages one person might not do the same for someone else. Cultural diversity and globalization are changing the workplace as quickly as technology. Honor the differences among your team members by offering them a variety of ways to learn and increase their engagement.

Learning Modes

While most of us learn by doing, by "getting our hands dirty," we all have different learning styles. Some of us prefer to read. Some like listening to audio tapes. Others learn by watching videos. And all of us might benefit from Lunch and Learn sessions, or One-on-One meetings.

Integrated Learning

Some years ago, it was common for employees to attend external training programs where, it was hoped, they would pick up something, even one idea. This is a very expensive way to go about learning.

Integrated learning is a comprehensive approach whereby you can make desired skills an integral part of your hiring, training, feedback, coaching, performance appraisal, and promotion systems.

Training and Learning Opportunities

Measuring Engagement Results

By using Organizational Engagement Surveys on a regular basis, you can correlate levels of engagement and morale with results in three categories.

Choose the category most appropriate for your organization: 1) top line results such as revenues or customers served; 2) Human Resources data such as attendance, injuries, lost time, sick leave, and disability premiums; 3) customer satisfaction surveys, quality measurements, contribution measurements, 360 Degree Assessments, and the ability of your organization to attract talent.

The results from these surveys can help you determine where and how to focus your training and learning resources.

12. Provide Proper Tools and Resources

Character Connection

Cognitively speaking, this **Leadership Engagement Behavior** would seem obvious. Unfortunately, it isn't. Technology is changing faster than ever before in history. The challenge for leaders is to keep abreast of actual needs versus wants, and then provide the right tools in order to facilitate the full engagement of their employees.

Getting Results?

Technology is a tool, and like any tool, applications vary. While some organizations spend exorbitant sums for systems they hardly ever use, others have employees struggling to get their basic work done because their current systems can't handle the volume or the applications, or both.

Your job as leader is to find out from your team if they have the tools they need.

Beyond the Bytes

By *tools* and *resources*, however, we're not just referring to computer software, BlackBerrys, and loads of server space. Here these terms are to be taken broadly, as one encompassing all the available processes for understanding and measuring development and engagement.

Engagement is a loop that exists between leaders and direct reports. So, in a sense, your tools as a leader are those of your team members as well. Such is the beauty of engaged interaction between people.

One-on-One meetings are the perfect way to discover who is struggling and who isn't, and group discussions will help you find out where the problems lie among the team and its processes. In either case, you have an opportunity to engage your people by equipping them to do their jobs better.

But there is more good news. A great variety of tools exist, including positive and constructive feedback, to equip you with ways to engage yourself and your direct reports, so that all of you can act on your engagement energy and deliver results together.

Let's take a look.

Leadership Communication Technique	*Intention of the technique*	*How to use the technique*
Mentoring	To help a person with ongoing career development The person does not necessarily report to you	**Over a period of time** • Very interactive • Both people responsible to track progress
Feedback Positive	To reinforce and recognize good performance At any point throughout the **Performance Management Cycle**	**Immediate, timely, sincere & specific** • **Observation, Impact (O.I.)**
Feedback Constructive/ Developmental	To target the gap between expected and actual performance in order to create an action plan for improvement At any point throughout the **Performance Management Cycle**	**Formal discussion** • **Observation, Impact, Query, Action (O.I.Q.A.)** • Requires solid performance data • Two-way discussion • Both people responsible to track progress • First discussion–may lead to Progressive Discipline if gap continues
Teaching/ Training	To help a person acquire additional knowledge or skill in order to do their job	**Teaching Steps (skill training)** • Demonstrate the task at normal speed • Repeat slowly, step-by-step • Let the person perform the task • Person practices • Watch the person complete task • Recognize as appropriate
Delegating	To help add a new task or project to a person's workload	**Review the following:** • Outline the task or project • Identify scope, level of authority, milestones, budget, resources needed, people to involve, reporting responsibilities • Involve the person in creating a critical path including contingency planning • Identify the level of support required • Identify next steps
Directing	To address an urgent need to change behavior or have the person take action e.g. safety issue	**On the spot discussion** • Describe the current behavior • Describe the change that is needed (or complete yourself if urgent) • Explain why the change is needed (or in an urgent situation, explain later) • Thank the person for their cooperation
Coaching for Engagement Continuous Improvement, Excellence	To help a person develop the skills to assume more responsibility, to prepare him or her for the next job	**Shared Responsibility** • Leader and the individual determine the goal(s) • Leader coaches using an interactive (versus a) communication process • Both monitor progress

Take advantage of the full array of tools, resources, and methods that can help your employees to perform at a level that befits their character.

By first engaging their character, equipping them fully, and then following up on a regular basis, you will keep your team around, focused, and energized–to produce results!

Recap of Thoughts

Speaking of better jobs, let's look at yours. We have taken a detailed look at how you can more fully engage your team by practicing engaging behavior.

If the **Leadership Engagement Behaviors** seem a little daunting at first, you are in good company. True, meaningful change is difficult for most people. Leading by engagement requires you to dig deep and discover how to leverage your authentic character to maximum effect. This requires your intention, focus, discipline, and skill. And it requires a lot of heart. After all, you're not building a team just for yourself. Great teams are built on connections between and among all of its members, including the leader! So, if you're not in it together, you're not in it at all. Connect by creating opportunities for mutual respect to grow. Treat your team members as people first–with civility.

Putting It into Words and Actions

Ask yourself these questions:

1. Civility

Compared to the **CIVIL** definition (**Care, Involve, Value, Inform Listen**), how civilized is your workplace?

The Merriam-Webster's Dictionary defines civil thus: "adequate in courtesy and politeness."[9]

Is "adequate" enough for you and your team to succeed? If you believe that improvements could be made, what impact would they have on engagement levels?

2. Listening

How well does the leadership listen to the workforce?

Are there improvements that could be made to encourage a more open, receptive way of listening?

What would the benefit be to your workplace?

What would the impact be on engagement levels?

3. One-on-One Conversation–Discussion Points

In chapter four, Respect Yourself, we discussed the importance of One-on-One Engagement Conversations and how the **Character Model** can be applied to them to gain a greater understanding of their impact. Below we look at how, with specific questions, you can carry out these "sit-downs" to maximum effect and benefit.

Remember–for every question share your own perspective as it relates to this person.

Do you believe that you're treated in a consistently civilized manner?

Do you believe that I'm honest with you? Do you believe the rest of the leadership is honest with you? Do I listen openly to you? Do you feel heard?

Do you believe that I/we are ethical in our practices?

Are you enjoying the environment?

What more autonomy would you appreciate?

How clear are your performance targets?

Do you feel that you're receiving appropriate positive feedback?

Am I dealing with performance gaps appropriately?

What if we make a pact to routinely offer each other a balance of positive and constructive feedback in order to continuously learn from each other?

What can be done to provide more significance in the job for you?

What learning opportunities would you like to explore? How are they linked to the organizational direction?

What tools and resources do you require to do your job more effectively?

4. The Leadership Engagement Behaviors

Perhaps now is the time to consider an organizational survey to assess how well the **Leadership Engagement Behaviors** are being practiced in your workplace.

You're invited to either download an audit to use with your team or explore our web-enabled Organizational Survey at:

www.centreforcharacterleadership.com/OrgSurvey.pdf

Your results will offer you some insight into where to better focus your engagement efforts, not only to build strong and engaging relationships, but to brace you and your team for situations that can threaten serious harm to retention levels and well-being.

As you will see in the next chapter, Harnessing Conflict, you will need a solid foundation to get through the times in your workplace when respect and engagement face some extreme challenges–among them, bullying.

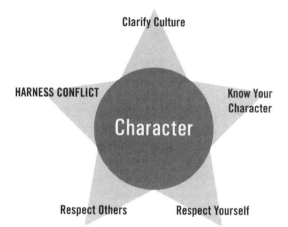

Clarify Culture

HARNESS CONFLICT

Character

Know Your Character

Respect Others   Respect Yourself

The intention of Harness Conflict is to explore how good conflict can encourage engagement, and how destructive conflict can lead to increased disengagement. We take a strong look at the notion of bullying in the workplace as it's an issue of significant importance which is loaded with potential for disengagement–or worse.

Harness Conflict shows how severe and negative behavior can put your character to the test and challenge your ability to attract, retain, and energize your team.

Intentional Acts of Character
The Leader Who Fought "Fire" with "Won't Fire"

Joanne worked for a manufacturer for over thirty years, through several buy-outs and a take-over. Sixty years old, she had contributed to the company and hoped to work a few years more before retiring. Then, a new president came to the company and began making negative comments on Joanne's work whenever her name was mentioned. Shortly thereafter, she developed a serious illness and needed time to seek medical care. The president directed Joanne's boss, a manager, to fire her, but the manager refused, stating that her work was sound and firing her during such a time would be clearly inhumane. A tussle ensued and went on until the human resources department stepped in and presented the lawsuit in the making. There has been a pallor over the career of Joanne's boss ever since.

Harness Conflict

With Fred Faber

> *Talent is formed in solitude; character is formed in the stormy billows of the world.*
>
> **Johann Wolfgang v. Goethe**

Conflict exists in the workplace. Engagement doesn't mean perpetual harmony. Sometimes conflict is good, as it results in creative approaches or reveals issues that should be resolved.

Conflict is often destructive, however, as a leader you will need to know the difference. Though we have discussed the signs of poor engagement and what you can do to remedy it, there will be times when you find yourself having to deal with issues more grave than a shortfall in monthly sales figures.

As a leader, you need to know how to handle individuals who are bent on being nasty, who have axes to grind and who have hurtful agendas. You need to know how to deal with differences of opinion, intention versus impact, gossip, bullying, and harassment.

After all, if you're going to get engaged, you want the relationship to work. So what are the forces that can seriously threaten the marriage?

In the last few years, we have recognized that there are different types of conflict–on a continuum they can be identified as moving from healthy to unhealthy. Unhealthy conflict can result in behaviors that are commonly and collectively referred to as workplace bullying, which can destroy your employees' morale and engagement, if not your company.

Differences of Opinion

Differing perspectives are good. If everyone in your workplace saw everything the same way, you would risk mediocrity and losing your focus on reality. As we saw in Character–The Core, "moderate engagement" is not the way to achieve sustainable success.

Engaged employees invest a lot of thought, feeling, and effort into their work. They're passionate, committed, and energized to perform at their best. Therefore, it's understandable that when differing opinions arise, the emotions of all concerned can get stirred up.

When you and your employees are working from within the **Character Model**, your team will be able to harness situations of conflict by behaving at their best while bringing forth their best ideas.

What makes differences challenging, and potentially engaging, is how they are discussed. So often someone will bluntly assert "you are wrong" or "you missed the point," an approach which smacks of the win-lose mindset and will discourage creativity and collaboration.

The better strategy involves better words: "Another way to look at this is…" or "an alternative to consider is…" or "I have had a different experience."

Pay attention to how your employees express differences. A simple change in wording can yield a win-win outcome.

Intention versus Impact

You see and interpret the world through a lens forged by your own background, education, experience, and state of mind. This means you may receive words or actions in ways that were not intended (apply **SNIP** before reacting!).

Misunderstandings cut both ways. If you can get it wrong, so can others when you are speaking or taking action. This ever-present possibility speaks to the need for ongoing, open communication.

REALITY BITES

The Path to Engagement Is Not Paved with Intentions Alone

Paul leads a team of customer service providers, with whom he holds weekly meetings. The service providers are an exuberant, high energy group, and Paul struggles to ensure that their meetings are structured, focused and productive. One day Marie, Paul's leader, called his direct reports and asked them how Paul could improve his effectiveness in the meetings. She received an abundance of information. Pleased, Marie then called Paul to provide the information. To her dismay, he became angry. He was stunned that Marie had taken this step without his knowledge; he felt undermined and humiliated. When Paul tried to tell Marie the impact of her actions, she kept insisting "my intention was just to be helpful." She wouldn't hear or acknowledge the impact of her actions. Paul's trust in Marie was damaged.

The ability to acknowledge the impact of behavior rather than simply focus on our intentions requires courage and authentic character.

Character is also required when dealing with the heavier, more potentially damaging challenges that may come your way.

Gossip

Gossip, which is defined as "to tell rumors or personal or intimate facts about other people, especially malicious,"[1] deserves special mention.

Boiled down, gossip is a form of manipulation, or even bullying, in which the gossiper attempts to change the way you feel about another person, for the worse.

Often, the gossiper intends for you to see them as the victim and a third person as the persecutor, which can land you on the **Karpman Drama Triangle**. And we know how that can hurt.

If gossip influences how you think, feel, and act towards someone, not only have you let yourself be manipulated, but you have lost your freedom of choice and misaligned your own intentions. Your character suffers.

To paraphrase Stephen Covey, your ultimate freedom lies in your power to decide how you will be affected by events outside of you.

Recall chapter four, Respect Yourself. Remember, you have the power not to become "the monkey in the middle." The appropriate response to a gossiper is to ask: "Did you let the person know your reaction?" Or "have you talked to them about this?" Often the alleged persecutor has no idea of the situation. Encourage the gossiper to speak directly with the person involved and you will stay off the nasty **Karpman Drama Triangle**.

Gossip as Bullying

It's not just petty chitchat. Gossip is bullying when negative stories are being circulated in order to hurt, embarrass, or control a person; or when they are intended to damage a person's position within an organization.

You are never going to stop people talking about others, but you can ensure two things: that you don't participate in destructive, bullying conversations; and that you hold people accountable for doing so.

There are times, however, when bullying occurs in a way that makes it difficult to hold the offender accountable. Obvious bullying has a quiet sibling and its name is passive-aggressiveness.

REALITY BITES

The Smiling Bully

She walks up to you with a smile. In the guise of an innocent exchange or a cordial conversation, she deals a blow in the form of information she knows will be hurtful. It may be an inappropriate demand, a bit of cruel criticism masquerading as a compliment, or perhaps a bit of bad news prior to your presentation. Whatever its manifestation, it's bullying with a veil, behind which lurks a mean message: I'll get what I want, be unfair, be disrespectful, and do it in a way that's hard for you to respond to. You're left stewing in your thoughts, feeling tense, and unable to respond or salvage your inner calm, while she saunters off, chortling with self-satisfaction at the harm she has inflicted. This is passive-aggressive bullying.

What makes this form of bullying so insidious and damaging is that it's delivered indirectly, leaving the targeted individual without overt cause or justification for recourse. Also described as "the wolf in sheep's clothing," the "iron fist in the velvet glove," or "damning with faint praise," bullying of this sort is a challenge for many people in many work environments.

So, how do you respond to this particularly sneaky, disarming brand of bullying? Peggy Grall, author of *Just Change It*, warns against taking a passive approach in dealing with bullies, reminding us that a passive reaction will only invite more aggressive behavior and leave you feeling resentful. The key here is to shine a spotlight on the behavior, to reveal the harmful intention behind the smiling face–what needs to be changed.

Here is Peggy Grall's Three Step Approach to dealing with passive-aggressive behavior:

1. Begin by gaining perspective on what happened. Speak privately with a trusted advisor. Consider the following:

    - Is there anything that you're doing that might be inviting this kind of behavior from others?

    - Could you be exaggerating what happened?

- Is it time to confront the person, or should you ignore this one situation and wait to see if it's a recurring theme?

2. Speak Up. Here you can use the **O.I.Q.A.** approach in an assertive manner.

   - **Putting It into Words** might sound like this:

   "I'm not comfortable with how you've just spoken to me. I'm certainly willing to consider your request, but there will need to be an understanding of mutual respect and clear language if we are going to work together."

   "I hear the request in your message. I want you to know that I consider it only a request and we'll have to negotiate what I am going to do (or pay, etc.). Here's what I need to clarify before making a commitment. What can you do in the future so issues like this are dealt with more consultatively and directly? What I'll do in the future is let you know immediately and directly if this type of behavior reoccurs."

3. Follow up. If the behavior changes, recognize the change using **O.I.** But if it continues, speak up again. This time explain the consequences of continued bullying behavior. If it still continues, execute the consequences.

Here are some possible consequences:

- You take the (bullying) issue to a safe place in the organization: Human Resources, your leader's leader, etc. Inform the offending person of your actions.

- A final step would be to choose to maintain a "dignified distance" from the person. Minimize your interaction, but continue to speak up whenever you are treated inappropriately. If you think this may be a case that will come to the attention of Human Resources, document carefully and rigorously.

You may be asking yourself why you should have to deal with bullying behavior at all. What's wrong with people that they feel the need to hurt people, cause woe, and take up our time and resources?

We know that bullying behaviors come from a place of insecurity and woundedness – even the 'polite' variety we've been discussing here. Peggy summarizes the issue as "hurt people hurt people." As we'll see in chapter seven, Build Trust, bullying lies in a dark zone outside the **Character Model**, far from engagement.

But, regardless of *why* a person behaves badly, the response should be the same: Bullying is unacceptable. Calling out the behavior floods light on the situation and may be the opening the perpetrator needs to consider his (or her) character. If he does, then everyone wins.

To win against bullying you'll require what we know is the glue of character–discipline. In all cases of bullying, remember that you'll need to draw deep to keep your balance and stay strong, as bullying is pervasive and powerful, and its consequences can be dire.

Bullying and Fear in the Workplace

Leaders can experience bullying as can all employees. Inappropriate behavior is destructive, no matter who the perpetrator is.

In April, 1999, a bullied worker went on a shooting rampage at OC Transpo, the Public Transit System in Ottawa, and murdered five people. The resulting coroner's inquest recommended that federal and provincial governments create legislation to prevent workplace violence, and that employers develop policies to address violence. In January 2001, the Canada Safety Council suggested that national laws be passed to execute the recommendations from the inquest.

Case law has started to address the issue. A recent Ontario Superior Court decision recognized that an employer owes a duty to its employees to provide a decent, civil and respectful workplace.

Over the past decade, workplace bullying has become an internationally recognized occupational health and safety issue. Prevention of bullying is one of the objectives in the European Commission's strategy for health and safety at work. Many European and Scandinavian countries, including France, Germany, Italy, Sweden, Spain, the Netherlands, and Norway, have introduced regulatory responses to the problem. In the United Kingdom, Ireland, and Australia, the courts currently address bullying under existing legislation. In the United States, workplace bullying is not yet recognized by the legal system, although a few states have initiated bills.

A 1999 International Labour Organization (ILO) report on workplace violence emphasized that physical and emotional violence is one of the most serious problems facing the workplace. The ILO definition of workplace violence includes bullying, describing it thus:

"any incident in which a person is abused, threatened or assaulted in circumstances relating to their work. These behaviors would originate from customers, co-workers at any level of the organization. This definition would include all forms of harassment, bullying, intimidation, physical threats/ assaults, robbery and other intrusive behaviors."[2]

REALITY BITES

Beer Bullies

When a supervisor in a beer manufacturing company caught one of his staff drinking beer in the locker room at 6:00 a.m., he sent the person home. An hour later beer production crawled to a snail's pace. Some of the employees were punishing the supervisor for holding the man accountable for his breach of conduct, causing the results from his shift to suffer considerably. Fortunately for the supervisor, his own leader supported his actions and deemed his decision appropriate.

In Canada, the province of Quebec, in 2004, passed the first anti-bullying legislation in North America.

The new Quebec law defines psychological harassment as *"any vexatious behaviour in the form of repeated and hostile or unwanted conduct, verbal comments, actions or gestures that affect an employee's dignity or psychological or physical integrity and that results in a harmful work environment for the employee."* Canada Safety Council [3]

While the previous **Reality Bite** looked at bullying behavior meant to intimidate a leader in retaliation for a decision he made, which is bad enough, there are other forms of threatening behavior.

Harassment, which is different from bullying, is defined as targeting aspects of an individual over which they have no control: ethnicity, gender, age, etc. This form of behavior is uniquely heinous in that the individual at the receiving end has an aspect of themselves which may make him vulnerable to be targeted.

In all their ugly manifestations, bullying and harassment take their toll on us inside and outside the workplace. What is the cost, financial and otherwise?

Costs of Bullying Behavior

Though workplace bullying has probably existed since the dawn of employment, our awareness of its full social and monetary impact has only just begun. Despite its prevalence, bullying is often misinterpreted as tough management necessary in our competitive world. Even by this misguided reasoning, however, outcomes construed as wins are Pyrrhic victories, as they come with too great a price tag.

In the United States, according to one study, bullying behavior and workplace stress cost businesses more than $300 billion annually due to absenteeism, turnover, workplace accidents, and other interruptions and inefficiencies.[4]

Further effects are felt in the form of checking out or poor performance, as bullied employees will hide from their tormentors, make errors, slack off, take longer breaks and unnecessary sick days.

While the effects of bullying on the workplace can be quantified in terms of time and money, the ultimate social, cultural, and spiritual impact of bullying on the human race may be immeasurable–genocide.[5]

This is strong subject matter, not to be taken lightly. So it behooves all of us to understand bullying and what it looks like in the workplace.

So Just What Is Workplace Bullying?

Well, almost all definitions of bullying include the following components to the behavior: targeted, deliberate, hurtful, ongoing disrespectful behavior for one's own gratification and is based on a power imbalance which is either real or perceived.

Bullying Behaviors

- Gossiping–spreading rumors
- Unfair criticism of a person's work
- Withholding information
- Consistently withholding recognition
- Excluding/Isolating
- Copying people on e-mails inappropriately
- Making fun/ridiculing
- Name calling
- Revealing someone's secrets
- Damaging someone's property
- Cyber bullying–postings on Facebook, YouTube, etc.
- Put downs
- Shaming
- Intentionally causing hurt

TWO REALITY BITES

The Bank and the Basketball Team

A former London England based Deutsche Bank employee who accused colleagues of bullying her won more that CDN$1.7 million plus at least $750,000 in legal costs from her company in 2007. The employee said she was subjected to "offensive, abusive, intimidating, denigrating, bullying, humiliating, patronizing, infantile and insulting words and behaviour."[6]

New York Knicks coach Isaiah Thomas was ordered to pay $11.6 million to former team executive, Anucha Browne Sanders, after a jury ruled that Thomas had subjected Browne to two years of insults and sexual advances.[7]

Who Is Affected by Bullying Behaviors?

Workers, supervisors, bosses and organizations all suffer. A study by Harvey and Hornstein found 90 percent of employees suffer workplace bullying at some time in their career and 20 percent on any given day–and that was in 1996.[8]

Two years earlier, in November 1994, the Institute of Personnel and Development (IPD) published the results of a survey revealing that one in eight (around three million) United Kingdom employees have been bullied at work in the past five years. Over half of those who have experienced bullying say it's commonplace in their organization, and a quarter of them say it has gotten worse in the last year. These figures are backed up by survey after survey.[9]

REALITY BITES

I have met many people who have told me that if someone isn't "nice" to them, they are totally defenseless. Why? They don't possess a range of responses to effectively deal with harshness. Whether their inability is due to innate qualities or upbringing, or both, individuals such as these are ill-equipped to deal with those who may wish them harm. They are vulnerable to bullying–they are potential targets.

If everyone in the workplace was well-intentioned and had great communication skills, it might work out for the defenseless person. But, as we all know, there are people who are not well-intentioned, who are not of "good character." These people, for whatever reason, have no intention of being civil or fair with their co-workers.

It is incumbent on all of us to recognize different approaches and adjust our style from passive to assertive to respond appropriately.

Of course, anyone who has spent any time as a child in a school yard knows about bullies. It's not a brand new phenomenon. So where have we been until now?

Why Is It Now Such an Important Issue?

Media hype, school and college shootings, workers going "postal," and kids learning behaviors in the school yard that they later take into the workplace have all resulted in lost productivity, new legislation, and new company policies and procedures. But the main reasons workplace bullying is such a hot topic is that it affects so many, its impact is so powerful, and yet it can be stopped!

If we can get employees to change the behaviors that rewards the bully, the pattern can be broken–and most studies say 80 percent of workplace bullying comes from the bosses![10]

Recall the brutish sales manager in the **Reality Bite** "Office Bash" in chapter two, the fellow who berates, derides and mocks his sales team in the weekly meeting? Here is a clear example of bullying that is a pattern on the fast track to becoming a toxic organizational culture.

As a leader, you are in a position to change your own behavior in a way that has a positive impact on others. Also, you must address bullying behaviors and actions carried out by members of your team.

It is your responsibility as a leader to harness conflict, to deal with bullies and bullying.

What If We Just Leave It Alone–Won't Our Employees Mature Through It?

Two leading researchers in Canada, Debra Peplar at York University and Wendy Craig at Queen's University, have shown what happens when school yard bullying is left unaddressed. There is no reason to think that workplace bullying can resolve itself either.[11]

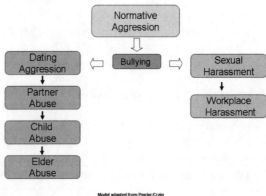

Bullying Power and Aggression in Relationships: A Lifespan Problem

Model adapted from Pepler/Craig

Why Is Dealing with Bullying Behaviors Such a Problem?

- There is the question of "put up with it or shut up" (an outdated way of thinking!).
- You need to learn how to have that difficult conversation.
- Whistleblower legislation is there, but it's hard to point a finger at a co-worker or "tell" on a boss.
- You might be called a racist, sexist, too sensitive, etc.?
- You're not sure if going to the HR department will help or hurt.
- How do you deal with it when there is no HR department?

Perhaps if more children experienced programs like Roots of Empathy, as we saw in chapter four, we wouldn't need so much legislation or so many formal measures in place to deal with bullying behaviors.

But, as we know, the world and the workplace are both imperfect places. This is why we need people like you.

So, how do you go about it?

Managing Bullying Behavior

He who trims himself to suit everyone will soon whittle himself away.

Raymond Hull

Being a person of character doesn't mean that you are constantly "nice." It means that you choose to do what is right for the situation. And if you're even nicer and more acquiescing to a bully, then you have sent a message that bullying reaps rewards, which can leave your team vulnerable to destructive behavior down the road. This is hardly leading by engagement.

Now, we are aware that people and personalities vary, and not everyone will deal with bullying with the same level of courage and proficiency. Also, no matter who you are, distinguishing between forms of conflict and deciding how you will approach the difficulties that arise takes practice–it takes courage and character.

Use the **Character Model.**

Character Strategies to Reduce Bullying Behavior

Intentions

Beliefs

- To accept that it's your responsibility to notice and deal with bullying behaviors
- To believe that bullying is disruptive, disengaging, and potentially destructive
- To believe that dealing with bullying behaviors is always the right thing to do

Goals

- To change the behavior that rewards the bully to behavior that discourages bullying
- To determine how to measure your success

Thoughts

- Understand that bullying behavior can be perpetrated by anyone, in any direction.
- Consider various strategies for dealing with negative behavior.

Feelings

- Pay attention to your own words and actions when you're frustrated, angry, etc.
- Notice your reaction when treated in a manner less than civil.
- Notice the emotional state of others which provides cues to whether bullying behavior exists.
- Maintain the discipline and courage required to deal with bullying behaviors unflinchingly.

Behavior

- Speak up when someone treats you in an inappropriate manner.
- Confront bullying behavior when someone on your team is treated inappropriately.
- Listen to feedback when someone tells you that they or someone else have been treated inappropriately.
- Recognize the behavior for what it is.
- Focus on assertiveness skills, self-esteem building skills for yourself and your team.
- Build on your strengths.
- Take care of your physical and emotional health.
- Enlist support in a manner that supports all concerned (don't turn the person into a target).
- Become familiar with (or create) the formal complaint process in the organization.
- Seek and learn new methods of action.
- Most of all, take action. Silence is consent.

One highly effective form of action you can take is called **Restorative Practice**. This approach is a group one, which is appropriate given bullying can affect one individual or many in the organization. Another distinguishing characteristic of this method is that it focuses on the bullying behavior rather than targeting the person perpetuating the behavior, which is a mark of character in an organization's culture.

Restorative Practice

In **Restorative Practice**, all those affected by a wrongdoing are given the opportunity to be part of a peaceful resolution to conflict, often meeting face-to-face in order to gain common understanding of the impact of the behavior in question.

Restorative Practice involves working with the people who have harmed others and those whom they've harmed. Instead of demonizing the offender, attempts are made to understand what he or she was thinking when they chose offensive, bullying behavior.

Restorative Practice, which has its roots in long-standing aboriginal traditions, is now a worldwide movement that employs peaceful approaches to rectifying harm, repairing damaged relationships, and moving people toward peaceful coexistence.

To be clear, the foregoing describes an approach by an organization with a progressive or enlightened culture.

Unfortunately, many organizations aren't yet in a position to benefit from **Restorative Practice**, though it's a worthy goal for any group of people or company. In reality, some situations of bullying don't turn out well enough to restore functionality, never mind peace.

REALITY BITES

The Lost Art of the Apology

A long-term employee in a small office once told me candidly that she has never apologized to anyone in her life and will never do so. She even seemed smugly proud of her stance. She repeatedly tells people, "I am doing the best

I can," seeing only her intention and not the effects of her behavior on those around her. Understandably, her co-workers find her difficult and frustrating, particularly as she confronts them on the minutiae of their words and actions as she expects them to take responsibility for what she perceives as their shortcomings. The criticism flows one way. The worst of it is that no one is prepared to remedy the situation. It's an intra-organizational stalemate.

What a waste of time and energy for all concerned.

Our discussion of bullying isn't meant to scare you or, heaven forbid, depress you. Dealing with the stark realities of your workplace is an unavoidable part of your role as the leader. In fact, dealing with bullying behaviors is everyone's job. Where engagement is the goal, no one should sit by and watch harm being done to others.

Let's face it, if none of us are prepared to stand up and do the right thing engagement will never take root and grow.

If the myriad forms and outcomes of workplace conflict are making your head spin a little, take a breath and remember that at all times, you can use **SNIP** to stay steady, ready, and aligned, from the inside out.

Recap of Thoughts

No one can make you feel inferior without your consent.

Eleanor Roosevelt

In this chapter, we have looked at what many leaders seem to dread: conflict. However, it need not bring you down or destroy your hopes of engaging your team, so long as you lead according to your authentic character, with courage and honesty and respect for yourself and those around you.

Keep your wits about you. Learn to distinguish between healthy conflict and the various types of negative conflict in your workplace.

We have looked at gossip, bullying, and harassment, which will appear in as many forms as there are people and organizations. No one expects you to become an expert at dealing with bad behavior overnight, least of all us, as we have been dealing with leadership issues for several years and continue to learn, everyday. We know how difficult they can be.

So, here are some quick tips.

Learn to communicate directly and assertively. Start by using the **Observation, Impact, Query, Action (O.I.Q.A.)** model. Remember that bullies operate from a base of power, real or perceived. Respond to them in a firm, confident manner, and you disarm them.

When targeted, maintain your self-esteem and harness the support of trusted co-workers to counteract the power the bully thinks he or she has. Share your problem with trusted friends, without becoming a gossip. Keep yourself healthy and well rested, as you can always cope better when you are stronger.

If the above doesn't work, turn to the policies and procedures in place in your organization. Or, if matters become very difficult, turn to legislation enacted to protect people in the workplace.

Perhaps above all, remember why you chose to lead in the first place; what you tell yourself on the long lonely drive into work or in front of the mirror at the end of a long day. You lead to make a difference, to improve not only your lot in life, but also the working lives of those individuals who look to you for engagement, for help in making their contributions. They are relying on you.

Remember this when you're confronted with conflict, choose the right words and actions, and leverage your authentic character.

Putting It into Words and Actions

As we said at the outset of this chapter, the subject of bullying and other negative behavior warrants a fair degree of treatment as it's a significant problem in our workplace and society.

However, we also want to be clear that not all conflict is crisis: In some cases there are opportunities to sharpen performance and enhance team engagement. It gets down to how challenging situations are handled–what you do and say.

1. Good Conflict

Assess your organization by asking yourself some key questions:

How are differences of opinions presented in your organization?

Is the difference explored thoroughly?   Yes_____ No_____

Does the difference become a catalyst for a creative, collaborative outcome?   Yes_____ No_____

What can be done to encourage people to speak up with differing perspectives?

Putting It into Words: Capitalizing on Differences of Opinions

Throughout this book we have stressed that leaders of character choose the right words (and actions). This is even more crucial when opinions collide. What should you say, and how should you say it, in order to deal with differences?

Here are some suggestions:

"I see it differently."

"I have had different experiences."

"Another way to approach this would be..."

"Let's consider every possible option."

"What I've seen done successfully in the past is..."

Intention versus Impact

As we saw earlier in the story of Paul and Marie a mismatch between intention and impact can occur without a leader knowing it.

Ask yourself:

How often do you feel that your actions are received in a different way that you intended?

What can you do to enhance the understanding between intention and impact?

Putting It into Words: Discussing Impact

"I hear that you're surprised by what happened. I'd like to explain my intention. Are you open to hearing what I have to say?"

"Please tell me what it was like to be on the receiving end of this conversation (or event). What's your reaction? May we talk through my intention?"

2.   Fear in the Workplace

Fear is a powerful emotion. When it permeates the culture of an organization, fear can be an insidious obstacle to engagement.

Ask yourself:

How truthful are people in your workplace?

Are they reluctant to provide their insights and relate actual experiences to their leader? Are you?

If information is being diluted, what's the impact on problem solving and decision making?

What can be done to enrich the amount of information flowing in all directions?

What would be the benefit of that enrichment?

3. Bullying in the Workplace

Clearly, bullying behavior can be a powerful force in any workplace, one requiring the utmost discipline, courage, and honesty in the leaders of an organization. Character means not looking away; it means looking closely, no matter how unpleasant a responsibility this may be.

So, ask yourself:

Are there people in your organization who feel that they are bullied? By their leader? By their direct reports? By their peers? By their customers? Do you feel that you are bullied?

If the answer to any of the above questions is yes, what strategy can you put in place to protect yourself?

What can be done to create a greater sense of safety in your workplace?

Putting It into Words: Standing Up to Bullying Behavior

"I don't participate in this type of conversation. When the conversation is civil, I will participate."

"This is not the way I communicate."

4. Accountability – Owning Up to Errors

Doing your part as a leader to harness conflict is a mark of authentic character. However, your team members also have responsibilities, as we have discussed.

In cases of conflict, your employees must own up to errors and poor behavior. Otherwise, no measures you take will be effective in maintaining engagement.

What's the behavior in your workplace in taking responsibility when things go wrong?

Do people try and hide it or is it transitioned into a learning opportunity?

Is there something you can do to demonstrate effective behavior in this area?

Leveraging your authentic character to harness conflict can seem like heavy lifting–the most demanding aspect of leadership. Like all worthwhile endeavors, however, leadership by engagement is not always easy and quick, but it's worthwhile–because there is a reward.

In the next chapter, Build Trust, we come to the big payoff, the ultimate reason why we endeavor to lead according to our authentic character: to gain trust, perpetuate engagement levels, and to ensure the ongoing success of the organization where we lead.

In the Words of Fred Faber

When I was asked by Kathleen to contribute to this book, it caused me to pause and reflect on the journey of my career thus far–something that every progressive leader needs to find the time to do.

Following a thirty-five year career in public education, I had been contracted by one of the countries largest and most successful school boards to take on the role of Principal, Bullying Prevention Management, wherein my job was to coordinate the board's initiatives related to preventing bullying by adolescents within the school system.

I realized the problem was a complex one requiring a versus "whole" school approach–one that involved parents, teachers, secretaries, caretakers, and administrators as well as students. By partnering with social agencies, local police, and world class researchers, I began to further understand the scope of the problem–and how prevalent bullying is in the workplace as well. I also gained insight into what specific solutions would really make a difference.

As I started to research workplace bullying specifically, I quickly became aware that it is pervasive; that there is very little literature about how to deal with it; that it is becoming increasingly psychological due to new social networking sites such as YouTube, Facebook, MySpace; and that the cost of bullying in the workplace is increased absences, turnover, and, potentially, law suits.

Research indicated that the incidence of bullying decreases in environments where focus shifts away from punishing the individual to understanding the behavior and restoring damaged relationships. Understanding requires patience, which in turn requires character.

Apparent was the lack of consistent character leadership in the workplace, which raised some key questions. Why was it so difficult for leaders to engage their employees? Why, despite the many mission and vision statements stressing the importance of values, were so many people at work treated with such incivility? How could organizations cultivate character in its leaders? Part of the difficulty is that developing and maintaining character is a long-term endeavor, one requiring great discipline. This is no easy task.

Engaging through character requires a shift in norms and practices from a place where bullying can go unaddressed to a place where it is consistently challenged. Organizations must attract the "right people," and practice engagement behaviors when hiring new recruits, conducting performance evaluations, and offering promotions–in alignment with organizational intentions and values. In short, they have to cultivate authentic character and lead accordingly.

On a personal level, I knew that leading with authentic character means I must behave consistently, at work, at home, or anywhere in life where bullying exists. Only in this way could I (or anyone else) hope to create schools, workplaces, and societies in which dignity, civility, respect, and trust are the new norms.

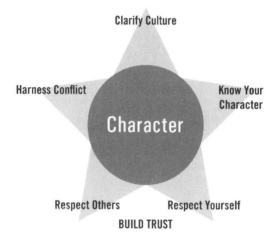

Clarify Culture

Harness Conflict

Know Your
Character

Character

Respect Others   Respect Yourself

BUILD TRUST

The intention of Build Trust is to highlight the relationship between trust
and sustainable engagement, to prove that high engagement and strong
levels of trust yield concrete, measurable results, and to underline that
we're not just talking about your employees trusting you, but about your
employees feeling that you trust them.

Build Trust shows that trust is both the result of higher engagement, and
the ultimate foundation for attracting, retaining, and energizing your team.

Intentional Acts of Character
David's Salon: A True Beauty

David is the owner of chi-chi beauty salon. It's a place where the patrons and the employees tend to be a well-groomed, fashionable lot, where one might assume the full diversity of society would not be welcome. Perhaps that would be the case if the owner were someone other than David. After putting the word out that he was in need of a new helper, David received a steady stream of résumés. There was no shortage of applicants, most of whom were young, pretty, and polished. He hired Sharon, who, like the others, was young.

What makes her different, however, is that she has an intellectual disability. Sharon talks loud, makes inappropriate remarks, and is less than flawlessly groomed. She's also the heart of the salon, says David. Not only do her co-workers treat her like the special, delightful person she is and include her in social activities, but the patrons embrace and enjoy her. As a leader, David could ask for no better employee than Sharon, who shows up to work on time, puts her heart into her work, and rarely, unless absolutely necessary, calls in ill. Quite simply, Sharon is a star because everyone in David's Salon benefits from her employment–and David is a true leader because he acts with trust and character.

Build Trust

The best way to find out if you can trust somebody is to trust them.

Ernest Hemingway

The Penultimate Point of Engagement

We're almost where we need to be. We've looked at the needs of your organization and you. We've established the necessity of creating a team culture of character so that engagement can thrive and performance can soar throughout your organization. And we've shown how the **Character Model**, **SNIP**, and our other models can help you remain steady and engaged so that you can engage others, according to your authentic character, from the inside out.

Now, what would all of this be for if not to gain and maintain the trust of your team? This is why you work to build engagement through your authentic character–this is where, and how, you lead your team.

Trust

Trust is an emotion. We either feel it or we don't, and its existence matters, in two significant ways: that you are trusted by your employees; and that your employees feel you trust them. Both are necessary for organizational effectiveness and continuing engagement. What does this mean for leaders and how they engage people in the workplace, in functional terms?

Simply, trust is based on people doing the right thing, and being able to talk about it if it isn't perceived that way. Trust is working when leaders and their employees feel free to make decisions openly and in good faith.

Metaphorically, trust is like an organizational atmosphere, giving life to collaboration and making progress possible. Trust is both a process and an outcome: It grows over time, and yet is necessary at all times.

Has trust always meant the same thing? To gain a greater understanding of trust, let's go back in time.

In the Day

Trust in the workplace used to mean that if you worked hard and were loyal to your organization you would follow a natural route of promotions and perks before retiring at age sixty-five with a gold watch. It meant you would be "taken care of."

And then the world changed. Somewhere around 1985 the ground started to shift, as a combination of related factors revolutionized the way we worked and lived.

Words like restructuring, downsizing and right sizing, became the buzz words of day. People were "packaged off" like stale bread. And although it was no longer a social stigma to lose your job, the turmoil this massive shift created on personal, societal, and financial levels was tremendous.

Morale among longtime workers sank, and younger ones either shrugged off changes as inevitable or viewed them as evidence of a greedy and myopic workplace. Time passed.

Virtual Work World

The past twenty-five years have brought unimaginable changes. Unsinkable blue-chip companies have rocked, previously unimaginable technologies produced a boom, and work is being outsourced not only to other locations in North America, but to the world.

We are contracted to companies, subcontracted to others, and we contract people to work for us. The telephone, the internet and virtual workers have replaced offices, typing pools, and assembly lines. Work has transformed.

Now many people shun the life of a traditional employee, loath to "put all of their eggs in one basket," reasoning it is safer to build marketable skills and many revenue streams. As one downsized leader nearing sixty years old stated, "we don't have careers any more; we now have cash flow."

Some may argue that if the lifelong careers and loyalty are gone, how can we still have trust? And do we still need trust? Well, would you do without it in your personal life?

Trust is necessary in all facets of life. But today, the focus of trust in the workplace has shifted.

What Trust Means Today

Today, trust is built by transparency, authenticity and, indeed, character. It means people evaluate the credibility and character of their leaders, rather than adhere to a vague, general sense of faith in the ever-changing organization.

Do you embrace and practice the **Leadership Engagement Behaviors**? Do you pay mere lip service to values, or do you lead with the intention, discipline, and courage necessary for engagement?

There have been many times over the years when I have asked leaders about the organizational values listed on their websites or posted in their lobbies. Eyes roll and heads shake.

Perhaps these leaders feel as many do; that there is a gap between the values corporations profess and the behavior they actually tolerate. In the wake of the scandals at Enron Corp and WorldCom Inc., many employees, investors, and leaders have lost what faith they had in the corporate world.

In an article entitled "Regaining the public trust: two top business leaders discuss the deteriorating regard for corporate America and what can be done to win back the public's confidence," published in *Internal Auditor Magazine* in 2003, Bruce W. Fraser reported that nearly 80 percent of Americans hold business leaders in "low esteem."[1]

Interestingly enough, this value roughly corresponds to the percentage of employees who aren't highly engaged, as we saw at the beginning of the book. Indeed, it would appear a lot of confidence needs to be won back.

Cynicism has become pervasive, or even normal, and many of our leaders seem to have simply lost faith in people. Or, maybe some people think the current state of the workplace is as good as it gets.

REALITY BITES

A Piercing Message

Blue Banana, a chain body-piercing studio in Cardiff, Wales, fired an employee by text message–while she was off sick! The company defended it's actions: "We are a youth business and our staff are all part of the youth culture that uses (text) messaging as a major means of communication," said Ian Bisbie, a Blue Banana director in a statement emailed to the *South Wales Echo* newspaper. (Associated Press)[2]

Here is an example of how organizational culture, trust, and reputation intersect. In all likelihood that story will become part of the folklore of Blue Banana and affect the culture for a long time. Potential recruits may be young, but they may think twice about submitting their résumés. As for Mr. Bisbie's justification, well, the telephone is also a major means of communication: Would you propose marriage to your partner through it?

There is a time, a place, and a right way of doing things, and it's the way of character. If Blue Banana's actions were ethical, why did one of their directors find himself in a position of having to defend them in the press? Some of us must feel we can do better at creating workplace cultures where trust, respect, and civility are to be expected.

Though people do move from organization to organization, at times with alarming frequency, and absolute faith in "the organization" has diminished, we still do have places of work with direct reports and leaders. After all, no one can completely redefine the human element of work, no matter how much technology changes the way work is carried out.

But we can create a new future for ourselves through engagement and trust–the timeless ingredients in all truly successful human endeavors. No generation can do without respect and trust – period.

Trust, like this book, isn't an add-on solution. It is nothing less than the total effect of a leader's authentic character at work, a result achieved by the disciplined application of the **Character Model.** Trust is built from the inside out, with behaviors that are aligned with intentions, thoughts, and feelings.

If this all still sounds a bit daunting and complex, there is a straightforward way you can understand where you need to be to start building trust among your team members.

Taken together, all the elements of the character "core" we've developed throughout the book might be described as a circle within which engaging, proactive behaviors take place, outside of which disengaging, reactive behaviors take place.

Are You Inside or Outside the Circle?

Though engaging your employees through your character requires intention to begin and discipline to maintain, the question you have to ask yourself is simple: Do you want to be a reactive leader, behaving "outside of the circle?" Or would you rather lead from the inside, to build your team's trust in you and their belief that you trust them?

Character Inside and Outside
of the Circle

Reactive/Potentially Destructive

No Reflection

Victim Stance

Intentional/Constructive
Conscious Choice
Reflective
Proactive
Value Based
Disciplined
Powerful
Aligned
Accountable

Powerless

Defensive

Unconscious

Undisciplined

No Accountability

By referring to **The Circle of Character** graphic as needed, you can remind yourself where you need to be leading according to your authentic character.

Although the models and graphics in this book are new (with the exception of the **Karpman Drama Triangle**), the idea of character with respect to dark and light, or wrong and right, behavior is timeless and universal. Let's step out of the workplace for a moment and into the metaphorical wilderness.

Two Wolves

One evening an old Cherokee told his grandson about a battle that goes on inside all people. He said, "My son, the battle is between two "wolves" inside us all.

One is Evil. It is anger, envy, jealousy, sorrow, regret, greed, arrogance, self-pity, guilt, resentment, inferiority, lies, false pride, superiority, and ego.

The other is Good. It is joy, peace, love, hope, serenity, humility, kindness, benevolence, empathy, generosity, truth, compassion and faith."

The grandson thought about it for a minute and then asked his grandfather: "Which wolf wins?"

The old Cherokee simply replied, "The one you feed."[3]

In the context of our discussion, your "wolf" represents your proactive intention (for good) or default negative reaction–destructive thoughts and emotions. You have the choice of determining your intentions, aligning your thoughts, feelings, words, and actions in order to lead others to higher engagement or not.

The choice *is yours*. Will you wander in the dark, "outside of the circle," where your behavior is reactive and potentially destructive? Or will you keep your character in the light, "inside of the circle," where your behavior is aligned with your intentions–proactive, constructive, and building trust?

Do the right thing. Stay in the light.

Now, assuming you choose to lead from an aligned position inside the circle, which I think is a fair guess at this point, what is the pay-off of trust for you and your organization, in real terms?

High Trust in Leadership Produces Results

High engagement levels will exist where trust has replaced a culture of cynicism, apathy, and anger; and an engaged team will pay dividends in terms of energy, focus, innovation, productivity, and harmony, as your team members, no matter how diverse, will see and feel the benefits of character.

The principal payoff of trust in an organization is employee performance. In a research paper entitled "Trust and Breach of the Psychological Contract," Sandra L. Robinson wrote of the close relationship between trust in management and employee performance. Specifically, a breach of trust by an employer can result in distrust, dissatisfaction, and, in our words, disengagement. When employees perceive a breach of trust or "an inconsistency between the words and actions" of management, they lose confidence in their relationship with their managers. The result is a decline in motivation to contribute to the organization's goals–and a culture of cynicism and defeatism.

Interestingly enough, the study also found that those who had been routinely disappointed by management were more likely to search for negative patterns of behavior in all new managers, causing themselves to withdraw even more from a psychological place where trust can develop.[4]

People like our "bashing" sales manager, mentioned in chapter two, create negative, disengaging cultures by pushing the perceived likelihood of trust out of the minds of team members. Untrustworthy managers also push their employees out the door, in a manner of speaking, as we also saw in that story.

Not surprisingly, demonstrations of trustworthiness by a leader will result in employees wanting to innovate and contribute and, well, stick around.

Clearly, the other payoff of trust is higher retention. While some turnover is unavoidable, trust in leaders will keep your employees from seeking engagement elsewhere. If you will recall the BlessingWhite research in chapter one, you will remember that a high degree of trust between managers and their direct reports encourages employees to stay and become engaged in their work. People can't help your organization grow if they're not there.[5]

And engaged employees will be more inclined to commit to your organization as it evolves from one of primal fears and reactions to one where true power is measured in character, trust, and opportunity.

People will talk, but now in a good way. Your company will gain a reputation for being one of the "best," and will begin to attract individuals who share its cultural values and want to do their best work with your team.

Trust perpetuates trust.

REALITY BITES

Don't Get Blogged Down

Many CEOs and executives are venturing out to the web by starting up blogs or personal web pages in order to stay in touch with all stakeholders, including employees and potential recruits. While the blog can be a powerful tool for communicating and conveying the human side of your leadership, you should use this medium with care.

According to Debbie Weil, author of *The Corporate Blogging Book,* a controversial posting can foment a flurry of potentially damaging replies across the globe–utterly beyond your control. Not to mention the amount of time and energy required to deal with the fallout.[6]

Showing your human side is okay so long as it's the side you intend to show. Yes, courage in the face of risk is necessary in a leader, but recklessness is never advisable. You want to enjoy the ultimate benefits of engagement and trust, not see your reputation damaged by an ill-considered posting. If you're going to blog, do so in a way that aligns your messages with your organizational character.

After attracting the best people to your organization, make sure they *feel* valued and trusted.

Are They Feeling the Love?

TRUST

Okay, love is a bit much to expect of leaders or co-workers. Most would be happy to get to retirement after an engaging career, or careers, feeling satisfied with the time they have spent working–a worthwhile legacy to strive for.

Your team members will need some trust to help them get there. When people feel trusted, they feel encouraged to contribute and take the right risks for themselves and for the organization.

How many times have we seen distrusted, disengaged teenagers act out recklessly? Now, your people are adults, most of whom are (hopefully) past the stage of extreme acts or overindulgence for the sake of shock value. Adult apathy and misbehavior, in the context of work, will take the form of poor performance. We need to consider that.

As we said earlier, the focus of trust is changing.

In a new study entitled "Trust That Binds: The Impact of Trust on Organizational Performance," Dr. Sabrina Deutsch Salamon of York University and Dr. Sandra L. Robinson of the University of British Columbia examine what happens to collective performance measures when employees feel that managers trust them. According to the researchers, higher levels of "felt trust" correspond to increases in responsibility, sales and customer service."[7]

That is definitely worth feeling, and experiencing.

REALITY BITES

Patricia's Light Bulb

Patricia decided to enlist her team on a day of home building with Habitat for Humanity. Having reached a point of exasperation (as we saw in chapter one), she realized she needed a way to get to know her team better, to show her trust in them, and to keep leading them long enough to engage them.

Construction goals were determined for their work, people were paired off in teams, and training was conducted by the staff. The day got underway.

Some of Patricia's team took naturally to the tasks. Some, however, didn't. She began to worry that her attempt at team building through home building was a mistake. But then, something astonishing happened as the hours ticked by and progress was replaced by chaos: Her team members started to help each other! Some people buttressed their colleagues, helping fellow team members where they could, to keep the construction going. Even more remarkable was the fact that people came to her aid.

Patricia, so talented in her real life role, felt klutzy and inadequate trying to work with boards and nails. It was somewhat humbling for her to be helped by people she had constantly criticized. It would be an exaggeration to say that absolute trust was magically built that day. It was, however, the start of better understanding and empathy among them–a foundation for respect and trust to grow.

Think 360: Building Trust All Around

To build trust in your organization, build your authentic character–the core and foundation of trust:

1. Clarify the culture you are creating–ensure your systems, policies and practices enhance mutual trust.
2. Know your character and its alignment with the culture.
3. Respect yourself and ask yourself if you are engaged.
4. Respect others and their need to be engaged.
5. Harness conflict.

The result will be that you've created a foundation built on trust.

Strategies for Engagement

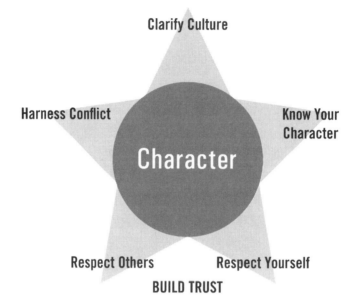

Maintaining Trust: Holding It All Together

Why build something only to see it crumble with neglect? Building trust is crucial for the sustainable progress of any organization, not to mention an amazing accomplishment. So, be sure your leadership and performance measurement systems are based on character and engagement.

Orbit of Trust: The Performance Management Cycle

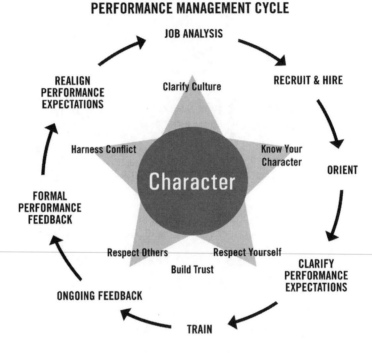

By applying the character-based **Performance Management Cycle** from recruitment right through every reach of your leadership, you will perpetuate trust and ensure robust engagement levels in and among your team members.

This last sentence warrants exploration. When we talk about engagement *among* the people in your organization, we are really talking about the atmosphere of trust, or what might be described as an **Orbit of Trust**.

Trust is like a 360-degree gravitational pull; it exerts a positive influence over people and their actions, building confidence and hope in the future. Build and maintain the **Orbit of Trust**, or the **Performance Management Cycle**, and it will help you build your organization.

While the essence and purpose of this cycle are universal, its specifics will vary from one organization to another. It will depend, in large part, on your organizational culture.

This brings us to an important point about the culture of engagement and trust: the language used by all team members to describe the leadership and themselves.

REALITY BITES

Who Are We?

The words we use in the workplace to describe ourselves reveal our intentions and beliefs regarding individual contribution and how much we trust one another. We've all heard the myriad descriptors for people in the workplace: boss, employee, superior, subordinate, staff person, temporary worker, contract employee, associate, team member, and servant-leader. All of these terms carry unique messages, conveying different attitudes about the relative importance of the various people in the organization.

When we use expressions like "he works under me" or "she is my superior" are we cultivating an environment in which people feel safe speaking up to power? Trust is about accepting the humanness of others and the value of their contributions (and that they'll endeavor to make them).

Sports teams, as we know, have coaches and players. The players are teammates, but so is the captain. Teams win when each player not only acknowledges the contributions of other team members but also values them. Whether you are an avid sports fan or a causal watcher, you will know that a small pass or throw can make the difference in leading to a win.

The most effective language honors the attitude that all contributions are not only valuable but necessary for the team to succeed. What if we are all colleagues, associates of the organization, or partners in an effort to achieve a goal? Yes, we have different jobs, but each of us is a leader in our own area of responsibility.

Naturally, the specific terms your organization chooses for the various organizational roles will reflect its culture. But when that language is one of inclusion, one that recognizes the importance of every person, you will create a level playing field of communication, one that encourages engagement and strengthens your team's **Orbit of Trust**.

While the language of engagement is foundational to building trust, be sure you mind the channels of communication within the organization.

Creating and maintaining a culture of engagement and trust means knowing how to communicate organizational goals, beliefs, and objectives internally. Just as leaders need to exercise due caution when using blogs and websites, so to do they need to use the email system wisely.

REALITY BITES

Emails Can Damage Engagement Levels!

We can gripe about it, delete it, try to ignore it, but the reality about email is that it is part of our working life–often a big part. The significance of its impact is made greater by the fact that this mode of communication (or miscommunication) is loaded with minefields. This is all the more reason for you to employ the **Character Model**, and an extra dose of empathy and discretion, when using email. Many of my coaching calls are based on second guessing the intention of the sender and developing appropriate next steps.

Here are some email best practices developed by a cross-section of companies:

- If it's a sensitive or urgent subject, talk directly.
- If you aren't sure of the meaning, talk directly.
- Reread all email messages before sending.
- Don't be surprised when a receiver interprets your email in a way you didn't intend. Talk about it.
- Beware of the copy/blind copy function. Only copy people if they truly need to know. Think about your intention with blind copy. Why are you really sending it?
- Put limits on when you send emails (lots of complaints I hear are about leaders emailing at 2:00 a.m.). Does this mean I should be working at that hour?

So you've done everything in your power to build trust and keep it going. You've aligned your intentions, thoughts, feelings, and engagement behaviors to create an organizational culture based on engagement and trust. Ideally, every situation going forward–from email to conversations to instances of conflict–should be dealt with according to the values, beliefs, and best practices of your organization character.

Unfortunately, not even the best intentions and actions will guarantee absolute trust or perfect outcomes throughout your organization, as we are all human. No one can control or predict how others will receive our intentions, words, and actions. And we can't overlook the fact that atrocious behavior by some people will put pressure on you to further define your character.

Even if you have a hand in some of the hiring at your company, some people may be beyond the direct reach of your leadership, and those whom you can influence directly may show you disappointing sides of their behavior over time, putting your character to the test.

To return to the quotation by Hemingway at the start of this chapter, people will reveal themselves when you trust them. Either way, good outcome or bad, you will come to learn the trustworthiness of the people in your midst.

So, how do we work with untrustworthy people?

How to Work with People You Don't Trust

REALITY BITES

Dignified Distance

Over the years, I've met many people who say that they're quite trusting of others, until something happens that demonstrates that the person isn't to be trusted. Lack of integrity, not listening to feedback, lack of empathy, failure to take responsibility for the impact of actions, and bullying behavior are key trust busters.

What to do when forced to work with people whom you don't trust? This is a significant question. While we hope our leaders will identify and confront destructive behaviors, unfortunately this will not always happen.

The best approach I've found for dealing with people whom one doesn't trust is the stance of "dignified distance."

In short, here's how you do it:

- Care about the person and treat him/her civilly.
- Identify the behavior that is causing the conflict.
- Apply the **Observation, Impact, Query, Action (O.I.Q.A.)** method.
- Recognize and reinforce appropriate behavior.
- Leave the door open to a closer relationship.
- Don't perceive the person as an enemy.
- Be available to help them develop a better relationship with you should the other person sincerely choose to do so.

As a leader, you will have to balance hope with realism. Always stay open to the possibility of building trusting relationships, and yet be strong and wise enough not to let distrust and negativity destroy the organizational culture, integrity, and reputation you and the other leaders have so diligently created.

Recap of Thoughts

Try not to become a person of success but rather a person of value.

Albert Einstein

In this chapter, we have looked at the grand organizational payoff of using the **Five Strategies**. By using the **Five Strategies** in a disciplined manner you will lead others through your authentic character, and cultivate engagement and trust among your team members. The collective result, the **Orbit of Trust**, will be one in which people speak and act with confidence in themselves and in the future–a successful future.

As always, however, you supply your own discipline and we'll supply the tips. Let's take a look at what you can do to create, heighten, and maintain trust in your organization.

Putting It into Words and Actions

1. Increasing Trust in Your Workplace

What is the trust level in your workplace?

How trusting are you of your leadership?

How does your level of trust affect your level of engagement?

Do you trust your people?

Do they feel that you trust them?

2. Adding to Your One-on-One Discussions

Do you feel that you are trusted?

What can I do to make you feel that I trust you?

Here's what I need to see from you to increase our level of trust.

What can I do as your leader to increase your level of trust in me?

3. Character Inside and Outside the Circle

What percentage of the time are you able to function inside the Circle of Character? (Proactively) ————%

Outside the Circle (Reactively)   ————%

What's the outcome of Inside the Circle?

What's the effect on your ability to build trust with others?

Is Your Character Outside the Circle?

What would you have to do to increase the amount of time that you're functioning Inside the Circle?

4. Creating a Benchmark for Your Leadership by Engagement Skills

An option for evaluating your skill level as a leader of character is to employ the Leadership by Engagement 360 Degree Assessment.

Your leader, direct reports, peers as well as you evaluate your skill in the **Five Strategies** of Clarify the Culture, Know your Character, Respect Yourself, Respect Others, Harness Conflict and the resulting Build Trust.

www.centreforcharacterleadership.com/le360.htm

I hope you've enjoyed **Leadership by Engagement**. Each day you lead will be filled with challenges big and small, and your learning curve, like mine, is likely an ongoing one. As long as you trust in yourself and lead with your authentic character, your journey will be upwards and rewarding.

We've looked at the urgent need for character and trust in our workplace, and how character is the core of leadership crucial for true and lasting engagement. We've looked at the bottom line impact that engagement has on organizations. We've looked at the need to build a culture of character and how doing so will have far-reaching effects on your organization. We've looked at the essence of character–respect–and how maintaining it makes your engagement and the engagement of others possible. We've looked at the foundation of character that will see you through difficult times in your leadership and help you harness conflict. And we've just looked at trust–the final outcome of engagement, a self-perpetuating atmosphere that will not only make your organization a better place to work, but will also ensure its longevity and success.

Of course, your success on a personal level will be that you will evolve and grow as a leader, not entirely free of stress (as this hope would be pie-in-the-sky nonsense), but one who can turn crisis into engagement and futility into possibility, and thereby leave a lasting and truly valuable legacy in the hearts and minds of those whom you have led.

Appendix

Recap of Character: The Models and Measures to Lead by Engagement

Leadership Engagement Behaviors

Research has revealed the 12 behaviors that will engage your team.

1.	Treat people in a consistently civil manner.
2.	Tell the truth.
3.	Listen openly with empathy.
4.	Conduct yourself in an ethical manner.
5.	Create an atmosphere of camaraderie.
6.	Provide autonomy to make decisions.
7.	Articulate clear, measurable, achievable performance expectations.
8.	Recognize contributions frequently, specifically and personally.
9.	Address performance gaps in a timely, private, problem solving manner.
10.	Provide opportunities for people to find challenge and significance in their work.
11.	Ensure training and learning opportunities are available.
12.	Provide proper tools and resources.

Character Model:

You are your character and your character is you. In order to behave as you choose, rather than just reacting, you must work from the inside out to illuminate, strengthen and align your words and actions. The layers of character are interwoven, interactive and interdependent. How well these elements work together will depend on who you are as a leader.

Your Character

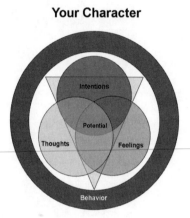

By Intention or By Default:

If you are allowing yourself to "just do what comes naturally" versus choosing consciously, you are in reactive model – a potentially dangerous place to be!

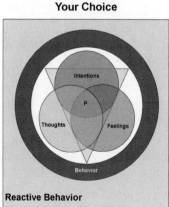

Strategies for Engagement:

The leadership strategies, with character at the heart and trust as the byproduct, help you focus your character on the job of engagement.

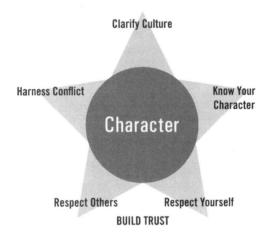

When you feel the flip it's time to SNIP:

SNIP helps you stay in control and aligned with your true intentions.

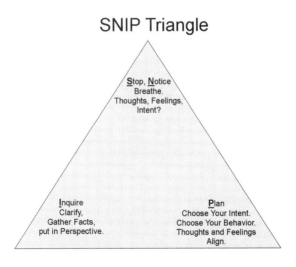

Best Opportunity for the Results You Want:

This controlled application of SNIP helps you leverage your authentic character and offers your best opportunity for success.

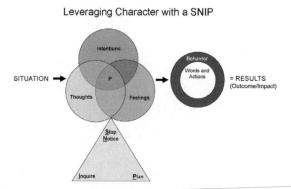

Orbit of Trust: The Performance Management Cycle:

Character and Engagement Strategies are central to your Performance Management Systems.

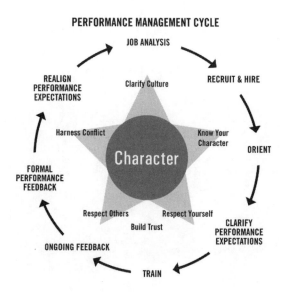

Receiving Feedback Internal Checklist:

Considerations   Communication Options

Is this information directly from the source, or is this person a messenger?

If the person is a messenger, suggest that the "source" needs to problem solve directly with you.

What is the intent of the speaker?

If the intent of the discussion is unclear to you, ask the speaker to summarize his/her objectives.

Do you believe it's possible to have a productive, two-way discussion with the person?

Yes → Proceed.

No → Stop the conversation and explain that you'd like assurance that your point of view will be heard and respected.

What credibility does this person have from your perspective? Do you believe that their perspective is well developed? Do they practice the behaviors that are being discussed?

Yes → Proceed openly.

No → Proceed carefully. Remain as objective as possible and think about whether this information could help you in any possible way.

Civilized Behavior:

Sincere civility is a basic requirement for leadership and success.

C	Care
I	Involve
V	Value
I	Inform
L	Listen

Connecting in Conversation:

Listening, hearing, and connecting through understanding and empathy is about asking rather than telling – about engaging the other person in the conversation.

Feedback Model: O.I.Q.A.

The model O.I.Q.A. (Observation, Impact, Query, Action) is a straightforward way to offer positive and constructive feedback.

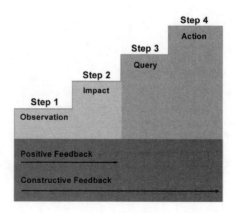

Integrated Learning:

Developmental opportunities can be found both on the job and independently.

Are You Inside or Outside the Circle?

Conscious or unconscious behavior: The choice is yours!

One-on-One Engagement Conversation:

Remember – for every question share your own perspective as it relates to this person.

Do you believe that you're treated in a consistently civilized manner?

Do you believe that I'm honest with you? Do you believe the rest of the leadership is honest with you/the workforce?

Do I listen openly to you? Do you feel heard?

Do you believe that I/we are ethical in our practices?

Are you enjoying the environment? What can be done to make the workplace more enjoyable?

What more autonomy would you appreciate?

How clear are your performance targets?

Do you feel that you're receiving appropriate positive feedback?

Am I dealing with performance gaps appropriately?

What if we make a pact to routinely offer each other a balance of positive and constructive feedback in order to continuously learn from each other?

What can be done to provide more significance in the job for you?

What learning opportunities would you like to explore? How are they linked to the Organizational Direction?

What tools and resources do you require to do you job more effectively?

What else is important for us to talk about?

How do we create action plans?

Monitor our progress?

How do we hold each other accountable?

Do you feel that you are trusted?

What can I do to make you feel that I trust you?

Here's what I need to see from you to increase our level of trust.

What can I do as your leader to increase your level of trust in me?

Glossary

Glossary	Page
360 Degree Assessments: A powerful method by which you as a leader can receivew feedback from all over your organization.	92,133,84
Authentic Character: Your intentions, thoughts, feelings, and behavior that are true to you and developed from the inside out, with reflection and self-awareness, so that you deliberately engage your team members.	8,24,29
Balance: Your ability to avoid manipulation by team members and thereby keep off the Karpman Drama Triangle and avoid becoming a Victim, Rescuer, or Persecutor.	30, 83,84
Beliefs: What you believe about leadership, engagement, communication, other people and yourself as defined by your principles and values.	23,35,41
Blink of a 'Y': The instant or pivotal moment in time in which an interaction between you and a team member can go well, toward engagement, or badly, away from engagement – depending upon how potentially strong emotions are handled.	128,129
Boundaries: The outer region of your Character Model (or Circle), beyond which will behave reactively, within which you will behave proactively.	75,80,105
Bridge of Understanding: The space between two people in which they will ideally meet each other halfway and come to an agreement.	82,83
Bullying: Any of a group of behaviors, including gossiping and harassment, in which one person attempts to gain power over another person by subjecting the person to disrespect, intimidation, or threats.	110,141,144
Caring: Your capacity and ability to value the well-being of others, to build engagement and trust among your employees.	17,32,106
Character Leadership: Your readiness, willingness, and abiwlity to master your thoughts, feelings, and leadership behaviors in order to align them with your intention to lead by engagement.	22,28,163
Character Model: The layered framework for understanding all the elements of oneself in order to lead yourself and others toward engagement in a fully aligned fashion.	24,33,53
Character Potential: Your greatest potential and ability to align and integrate your intentions, thoughts, feelings, and behaviors, to engage your team and thereby achieve the best results possible.	24,67,102
CIVIL: The definition of civilized behavior, which can help you manage your feelings so that you Care, Involve, Value, Inform, and Listen, so that you treat people in a consistently civil manner.	9,103

Glossary	Page
Civility: A key Leadership Engagement Behavior by which you demonstrate respect and common decency toward your team members.	102,104,113
Coaching: To help a person develop the skills to assume more responsibility, to prepare him or her for the next job.	115,116,135
Community: The society of people outside the organization that are still inextricably connected to it because of the people it employs, the products and services it sells, and the greater contribution it makes inside and outside the business environment.	38,115,130
Conflict: Any instance or condition in which two or more parties are at odds – sometimes positive and constructive, other times negative and destructive.	141,148,152
Cost of disengagement: The total cost poor engagement has on an organization in terms of absenteeism, stress leave, turnover, low productivity, and acts of bullying and sabotage.	4,33,173
Cost of turnover: The total cost of people leaving an organization before they have made a contribution above the investment an organization has made in them.	7,14,41
Delegating: To help add a new task or project to a person's workload.	135
Directing: To address an urgent need to change behavior or have the person take action.	135
Discipline: The essential quality in people that allows them to work toward their goals by using the Character Model from the inside out.	20,23,72
Empathy: The ability to see situations from another's perspective, regardless of whether or not you have experienced what they are experiencing.	24,107,109
Employee Engagement: The readiness, willingness, and ability of your team members to improve their performance and thereby achieve sustainable success for your organization.	3,9,14
Feedback: Information received with respect to one's performance – from any source.	49,80,87
Feelings: Powerful sensations that allow you to feel your emotions, providing information that can help you understand yourself, what is happening to you and to others around you; right-brain activity.	22,23,44
Fight-or-flight: The primal reaction in which the strong chemical response to a perceived threat causes a person to flee or fight.	63
Goals: Your priorities and objectives as regards specific situations in accordance with your beliefs and purpose.	23,39,131
Gossip: The creation and spreading of rumors or information intended to damage the reputation and standing of the person who is the subject of the rumor.	105,144,150

Glossary	Page
Inside the Circle of Character: The realm of your words and actions within which you behave positively, proactively and intentionally, in order to lead others by engagement.	171,184
Intentional Acts of Character: Actions or measures taken which demonstrate your character at work.	32,45,78, 100, 140,166
Intentions: Your purpose, beliefs, and goals as a leader.	23, 35, 60
Intuition: Your powerful ability to know "without knowing," by reading your bodily feelings in a situation.	63,71,73
Karpman Drama Triangle: The framework/model which helps you keep your balance by describing the negative relationships between Victims, Rescuers, and Persecutors.	84,91,96
Leadership by Engagement: Your readiness, willingness, and ability to leverage all facets of your authentic character in order to attract, retain, and energize employees that will achieve sustainable success for your organization.	8,9,20
Leadership Engagement Behaviors: The twelve essential, core leadership behaviors which if performed in a consistent and disciplined manner, will increase engagement in your team.	17,21,72
Legacy: The intended and lasting effect of your leadership that continues to impact others after you have left an organization.	23,49,130
Listen, Acknowledge, and Ask: An effective approach for listening to others with empathy.	107,126, 129
Managerial Stress: The strain and futility you feel when as you struggle to engage your team members while at the same feeling the pressure of accountability to your own leader and other stakeholders.	6,24,64
Manipulation: Any form of words or actions meant to keep another person off balance, to make the person act in a way they don't intend to.	75,80,84
Mentoring: To help a person (who may or may not report to you) with ongoing career development,	135
O.I.: Observation, Impact is the tool to help you offer positive recognition to your team members in a way that is less stressful or awkward for both parties.	122,135
O.I.Q.A: Observation, Impact, Query, Action is the tool to help you proactively carry out successful performance evaluations and developmental discussions with your team members, in a way which helps you avoid the negative path in the Blink of the 'Y.'	126,135, 146
Objectives: What you are trying to achieve at any given point in time, in one conversation or interaction.	23,39,119

Glossary	Page
One-on-One: The form of discussion between leaders and individual team members in which both parties communicate in order to gain mutual understanding of one another, deal with key issues and behaviors, cultivate trust, increase engagement, and improve performance.	93,118,194
Orbit of Trust: The self-perpetuating climate of trust among all team members and leaders in an organization.	178,183, 190
Organizational Culture: The predominant and collectively supported behavior within an organization which reflects commonly held beliefs and values.	32,50,57
Outside the Circle of Character: The realm of your words and actions outside of your Character Circle, where your behavior is negative, reactive, and not in alignment with your intention to lead others by engagement.	171,184
Performance Management Cycle: The entire cycle of leadership, from hiring to ongoing feedback, through which you and other leaders can perpetuate the Orbit of Trust and high levels of engagement.	178,190
Personality: Your total and inborn way in which you express your entire self, your entire character.	25,70,87
Principles: What you believe to be true and important.	23,35,51
Priorities: What is most urgent and important in planning your pathway to fulfilling your purpose or achieving your intended goal of better engaging your team members.	23,39,52
Proactive Behavior: Behavior Inside the Circle of Character, where your actions and words are positive and aligned with your thoughts and feelings, and your intention to engage your team members.	121,126, 171
Productivity: The individual and collective measure of employee contribution measured in revenue.	5,14,41,44
Purpose: The leadership legacy you wish to leave, that motivates you to speak and act; what you aim to achieve.	23,33,35
Reactive Behavior: Behavior Outside the Circle of Character, where your words and actions are negative and not in alignment with your thoughts and feelings, and your intention to engage your team members.	71,188
Recognition: Honoring and appreciating the contributions made by others and the qualities of their character that they leverage in order to make a difference.	83,120,150
Reflection: The deliberate, conscious act of assessing yourself, your thoughts, feelings, and behavior.	79,80
Respect: The fundamental belief that everyone in your organization is equal as humans and deserving of civil treatment and opportunities to become engaged.	12,18,79, 101
Responsibility (to others): Your ability to recognize and act upon your need to engage others.	43,83,111, 128

Glossary	Page
Responsibility (to self): Your ability to recognize and act upon your need to keep yourself engaged and free of manipulation.	5,80,96
Restorative Practices: The approach/process whereby bullying behavior is dealt with inclusively, so that all parties affected participate in understanding and stopping the bully behavior without attacking the perpetrator, so that the harm is addressed and the offending behavior corrected.	156
Results: The intended outcome of all plans and actions carried out to better an organization by moving it in the direction of engagement and sustainable growth.	4,14,27
Retention: The measure of an organization's ability to keep it's desirable employees engaged and energized.	6,14,15
Self-mastery: Your ability to use the Character Model in an ongoing, self-disciplined fashion, so that you continually align your intentions, thoughts, feelings, and behavior in every situation and interaction.	25,63,65
Self-respect: Your ability to ensure your own engagement and well-being.	75,79,95
Senior Leadership Team: All leaders who plan and participate in creating and maintaining an organizational culture of engagement through authentic character.	37,47,52
SNIP: The self-management tool that allows you to Stop, Notice, Inquire, and Plan as to how you will interact with others in a way that aligns your behavior with your thoughts, feelings, and intentions – so that you interact with others in the way that you intend.	64,73,75
Stress: The mental and physical manifestation of thoughts and feelings in the face of obstacles, challenges, or thwarted goals.	6,44,73
Teaching/Training: The process of helping others learn or acquire new knowledge or skills.	135
Thoughts: Your ability to reason, evaluate, and solve problems; left-brain activity.	23,42,61
Town Hall Meetings: The method of information sharing between you and your team members which often involves open discussion and Q&A in order to explore and understand common issues.	95
Trust: The emotion felt between and among humans that allows them to feel secure enough to find common goals and work toward them.	18,37,165
Turnover: The rate at which employees leave an organization after orientation and training.	14,27,41
Values: Your guidelines regarding how to treat yourself, your organization, and others.	20,23,36
Virtual work: All manner of work performed outside the conventional or traditional "brick-and-mortar" office environment.	13,168

Endnotes

	Character — The Core
1.	Engagement levels in Canada and the United States: Towers Perrin, Towers Perrin Global Workforce Study – Executive Report, *Winning Strategies for a Global Workforce: Attracting, Retaining and Engaging Employees for a Competitive Advantage,* (2005), page 8.
2.	Ibid., 10.
3.	Double-digit and single-digit growth companies: Hewitt Associates, *Research Brief: Employee Engagement Higher at Double-Digit Growth Companies* (2004): page 5. The study was done with Michael Treacy, author of *Double-Digit Growth: How Great Companies Achieve it no Matter What.*
4.	Productivity and Engagement: Watson Wyatt Worldwide, 2006/2007 Work USA Survey Report, *Debunking the Myths of Engagement* (2006/07), page 4.
5.	Buffet Taylor National Wellness Study 2000: *The Second Tri-Annual Buffet Taylor Wellness Study, from the web*: http://www.phac-aspc.gc.ca/pau-uap/fitness/work/trends_e.html
6.	This popular "alternative song by Depeche Mode, "Everything Counts," from their LP *Construction Time Again* (1983), decried corporate greed and corruption. We assert that workplaces can lower stress and be competitive by leveraging character of employees.
7.	Depression costs the United States: "ILO report examines mental health in the workplace in Finland, Germany, Poland, United Kingdom and United States," a press release dated October 10, 2000, in reference to a study called *Mental health in the workplace: Introduction,* Ms. Phyllis Gabriel and Ms. Marjo-Riitta Liimatainen, International Labour Office, Geneva, October 2000, taken from web: http://www.ilo.org/global/About_the_ILO/Media_and_public_information/ Press_releases/lang--en/WCMS_007910/index.htm
8.	Depression costs Canada: Dwayne Runke, *Canadian HR Reporter,* Toronto, July 16, 2007, Volume 20, Issue 13, page 22.
9.	Workplace stress, depression, anxiety, and absenteeism: Ipsos Reid, "Contributors to Workplace Absenteeism and Healthcare Benefits Costs," from the web, Ipsos News Center, March 18, 2004: http://www.ipsos-na.com/news/pressrelease.cfm?id=2089
10.	Managerial stress: WarrenShepell Research Group, *Managerial and Executive Stress: An EAP's Perspective* (2006), page 2.
11.	Daniel Goleman, Richard Boyatzis, Annie McKee, *Primal Leadership: Learning to Lead with Emotional Intelligence* (Harvard Business School Press, 2002), page 5.
12.	BlessingWhite, *Employee Engagement Report 2006 – Executive Summary* (2006), page 4.

Character — The Core *(continued)*
13. Daniel Goleman, Richard Boyatzis, Annie McKee, *Primal Leadership: Learning to Lead with Emotional Intelligence* (Harvard Business School Press, 2002), page 5.
14. Twice as many seniors as children by 2031: "Canada's Demographic Revolution Adjusting to an Aging Population," The Conference Board of Canada, March 2006.
15. Shortfall of 10 million workers age 25 – 44 by year 2010: Authoria, "Winning the War on Talent" white paper, U.S. Bureau of Labor Statistics, July 21, 2006, page 1.
16. Cost of turnover: William G. Bliss, Bliss & Associates Inc., "Cost of Employee Turnover," accessed on the web on January 27, 2008: http://www.isquare.com/turnover.cfm
17. Two top considerations when looking for work: Janis Foord Kirk, "The changing face of labour in Canada," Workpolis.com (in association with the Toronto Star), September 14, 2007, from the web: http://www.workopolis.com/work.aspx?action=Transfer&View=Content/Common/Ar ticlesDetailView&articleId=Star20070914File1Article1&lang=EN&articleSource=S tar&OldUrl= . The article references an Ipsos Reid study conducted for Sympatico/ MSN in July 2007.
18. Top three drivers of retention: Engagement levels in Canada and the United States : Towers Perrin, Towers Perrin Global Workforce Study – Executive Report, *Winning Strategies for a Global Workforce: Attracting, Retaining and Engaging Employees for a Competitive Advantage* (2005), page 5.
19. The importance of manager-employee relationships: BlessingWhite, *Employee Engagement Report 2006 – Executive Summary* (2006), pages 7 and 8.
20. Employees look for respect from managers: David Sirota, Ph.D.; Louis A. Mischkind; Michael Irwin Meltzer, *Sirota Survey Intelligence* (2005).
21. Canada and the United States share the same top engagement driver: Towers Perrin, Towers Perrin Global Workforce Study – Executive Report, *Winning Strategies for a Global Workforce: Attracting, Retaining and Engaging Employees for a Competitive Advantage* (2005), pages 17 and 23.
22. Perks alone will not inspire top performance: Gerard H. Seijts and Dan Crim, "What engages employees the most or, The Ten C's of Employee Engagement," Ivey Business Journal, March/April 2006, page 3.
23. The core of the Character Model: conation: Huitt, W. (1999). "Conation as an important factor of mind," *Educational Psychology Interactive*. Valdosta, GA: Valdosta State University, retrieved from the web on January 27, 2008: http://chiron.valdosta.edu/whuitt/col/regsys/conation.html.
24. Carl Jung's on personality: The Columbia World of Quotations, accessed on the web on January 27, 2008: http://www.bartleby.com/66/92/31792.html. The attribution on the Bartleby website: Carl Jung (1875–1961), Swiss psychiatrist. *The Development of Personality* (1934), repr. In Collected Works, vol. 17, ed. William McGuire (1954).
25. Change in the brain: Daniel Goleman, *Working with Emotional Intelligence* (Bantam, 2000): page 328.

Clarify the Culture	
1.	The importance of character leaders: James C. Sarros, Brian K. Cooper, and Joseph C. Santora, "The Character of Leadership," Ivey Business Journal Online, May/June 2007: http://www.iveybusinessjournal.com/article.asp?intArticle_ID=689
2.	Regional Municipality of York listed as one of Canada's top 10 employers: Mediacorp, *"Canada's Top 100 Employers," Maclean's,* October 2007.
3.	Four Seasons culture: Four Seasons Hotels and Resorts, Employment section of website, accessed January 27, 2008: http://www.fourseasons.com/employment/.
4.	Bad hires and promotions: *Right Management Survey 2006: The War For Talent,* Warren Evans, July 21, 2006.
5.	Happiest in a state called flow: *Mihaly Csikszentmihalyi, Finding Flow: The Psychology of Engagement with Everyday Life,* (Basic Books, 1998).
6.	Toxic emotions, destructive behaviors: Henry A. Hornstrein and Donald W. de Guerre, "Bureaucratic Organizations are Bad for our Health," Ivey Business Journal, March/April 2006.
7.	EQ tests and performance: Cary Cherniss, "Emotional Intelligence: What it is and Why it Matters," by Cary Cherniss, Graduate School of Applied and Professional Psychology (GSAPP), Rutgers University, 2000. This paper was presented at the Annual Meeting of the Society for Industrial and Organizational Psychology, New Orleans, LA, on April 15, 2000, as reported on the website for the Consortium for Research on Emotional Intelligence in Organizations: http://www.eiconsortium.org.

Know Your Character	
1.	The plastic brain: Dr. Norman Doidge, *The Brain Changes Itself* (Viking USA, February 23, 2007).
2.	Jobs on Jobs: Steve Jobs, as reported in the Stanford News Service, June 14, 2005, Stanford University: "This is the text of the Commencement address by Steve Jobs, CEO of Apple Computer and of Pixar Studios, delivered on June 12, 2005."

Respect Yourself	
1.	The importance of engaged managers: BlessingWhite, *Employee Engagement Report 2006 – Executive Summary,* (2006): page 7.
2.	Ted Rogers as "dicta-terrorist": Caroline Van Hasselt, John Wiley, *High Wire Act: Ted Rogers and the Empire that Debt Built* (John Wiley & Sons, 2007), page 309.

Respect Others
1. Incivility in the workplace: Robert Brooks et al., "Incivility in the Workplace," Public Virtues, in cooperation with Southern New Hampshire University Graduate School of Business, accessed on the web on January 27, 2008: http://www.publicvirtues.com/Incivility_Study.html#anchor25090176.
2. The need to feel understood: Maslow's Hierarchy of Needs. "A Theory of Human Motivation," Abraham Maslow, 1943.
3. Definition of Empathy: University of Minnesota, Office of Human Resources, accessed on the web on January 27, 2008: http://www1.umn.edu/ohr/profdev/definitions.html.
4. Roots of Empathy: The passage was taken from the Roots of Empathy (ROE) website, in the About Our Program section, under Emotional Literacy: http://www.rootsofempathy.org/ProgDesc.html.
5. Lisa Belkin, a journalist with the *New York Times*, cited research by Ipsos that found those whose managers have a good sense of humor are more likely to stick around than those whose managers lack a sense of humor.
6. Coaching: The International Coaching Federation, http://www.coachfederation.org/ICF/For+Coaching+Clients/What+is+a+Coach/.
7. Drucker on the "New Organizations": Peter F. Drucker, "The Coming of the New Organizations," Harvard Business Review on Knowledge Management, Harvard Business School Press (1998), pages 1–19.
8. Impact of Community Work: Paul Brent, "Great Places to Work, *The Toronto* Star, October, 2006: http://www.thestar.com/specialsections/top50/article/170121. The article refers to Anthony Meehan; publisher of *Canada's Top 100 Employers,* First edition, 1992.
9. The Merriam-Webster's Dictionary defines civil thus: "adequate in courtesy and politeness."

Harness Conflict	
1.	Definition of gossip: MSN Encarta Dictionary, accessed on the web: http://encarta.msn.com:80/dictionary_1861614749/gossip.html.
2.	Definition of bullying: Helge Hoel, Kate Sparks, and Cary L. Cooper, "The Cost of Violence/Stress at Work and The Benefits of a Violence/Stress Free Working Environment," a report commissioned by ILO, Geneva 1998, University of Manchester Institute of Technology, page 19.
3.	Definition of psychological harassment: "Act Respecting Labour Standards,"Sect. 81.18, June 1, 2004, accessed on the web: http://www.cnt.gouv.qc.ca/en/lois/normes/normes/harcelement.asp
4.	Costs of bullying behavior: Tracie Stone, "Bullying Grows as a workplace issue," New Hampshire Business Review Daily, June 8, 2007, accessed online: http://www.nh.com/apps/pbcs.dll/article?AID=/20070608/ BUSINESSREVIEW08/70606002/-1/BUSINESSREVIEW. The article refers to stress management experts at Virginia-based Inroads LLC.
5.	Bullying leading to genocide: Barbara Coloroso, *Extra Ordinary Evil, A Brief History of Genocide* (Viking Canada, 2007).
6.	Deutsche Bank employee, Reality Bites: Mick Hume, "When did good old-fashioned office politics become bullying?" The London Times, August 11, 2006, accessed on the web: http://www.timesonline.co.uk/tol/comment/columnists/mick_hume/article606204.ece.
7.	Anucha Browne and the New York Knicks, Reality Bites: Michael S. Schmidt and Maria Newman, "Jury Awards $11.6 Million to Former Knicks Executive," The New York Times, accessed on the web: http://www.nytimes.com/2007/10/02/sports/basketball/03garden-cnd.html
8.	Who is affected by bullying?: Harvey A. Hornstein, *Brutal Bosses and Their Prey* (Riverhead, October 1, 1997).
9.	Who is affected by bullying?: Elaine Douglas, *Bullying in the Workplace: An Organizational Toolkit* (Gower Publishing Ltd, 2001), page 5.
10.	Eighty percent of bullying comes from bosses: Gary Namie, *The Bully at Work: What You Can Do to Stop the Hurt and Reclaim Your Dignity on the Job* (Sourcebooks, 2000).
11.	Bully Power and Aggression in Relationships: A Lifespan Problem: Debra J. Pepler and Wendy M. Craig, "A Peek Behind the Fence: Naturalistic Observations of Aggressive Children With Remote Audiovisual Recording," York University, *Developmental Psychology 1995*, volume 31, number 4, pages 548–553: copyright 1995 by the American Psychological Association, Inc.

Build Trust	
1.	What trust means today: Bruce W. Fraser, "Regaining the public trust: two top business leaders discuss the deteriorating regard for corporate America and what can be done to win back the public's confidence," *Internal Auditor Magazine*, February 2003.
2.	Blue Banana, Reality Bite: Simon de Bruxelles, "*Sacking by text is just part of youth culture, says boss,*" UK Times Online, August 4, 2006: http://technology.timesonline.co.uk/tol/news/tech_and_web/personal_tech/article699952.ece.
3.	Two wolves: http://www.firstpeople.us/FP-Html-Legends/TwoWolves-Cherokee.html.
4.	Trust in management: Sandra L. Robinson, "Trust and Breach of the Psychological Contract," *Administrative Science Quarterly*, December 1996.
5.	BlessingWhite, *Employee Engagement Report 2006 – Executive Summary* (2006), pages 7 and 8.
6.	Don't Get Blogged Down, Reality Bites: Debbie Weil, *The Corporate Blogging Book* (Penguin Group, August 2006).
7.	Trust felt by employees: Sabrina Deutsch Salamon, Sandra L. Robinson, "Trust That Binds: The Impact of Trust on Organizational Performance," *Journal of Applied Psychology* (in press).

Centre for Character Leadership

in affiliation with
Redmond & Associates

Please visit our website for information on how to fully engage your team. Our coaching services, assessments and learning solutions have one focus: to attract, retain and energize the talented people of the workplace.

www.CentreforCharacterLeadership.com

Email: info@CentreforCharacterLeadership.com
Phone: 905-478-7962
Toll Free: 1-888-270-4205